LORD CASTLEROSSE
His Life and Times

LORD CASTLEROSSE
His Life and Times

George Malcolm Thomson

Weidenfeld and Nicolson
11 St John's Hill London SW11

Copyright © London Express 1973

ISBN 0 297 76624 4

Printed in Great Britain by
Bristol Typesetting Co. Ltd,
Barton Manor - St Philips,
Bristol

Contents

Illustrations

The author and publishers would like to acknowledge the following organizations for kindly allowing the reproduction of pictures in their possession: the Bibliothèque Nationale, Paris, for the photograph of Jacqueline Forzanne; Associated Press for the photograph of Lord Castlerosse's second wedding; Central Press for the photograph of Lord Castlerosse with the Prince of Wales; the Radio Times Hulton Picture Library for the photograph of Lord Castlerosse with friends by the sea and Lady Castlerosse with Mrs Hoffman; and London Express for the ten other photographs in this book. The author and publishers are grateful to Mr Antony Wysard for permission to reproduce his cartoon of Lord and Lady Castlerosse on the jacket of this book. The cartoon was first reproduced in *The Tatler* in 1929, when the artist was but twenty-one years of age, and is now in the possession of Mr Osbert Lancaster.

Foreword

I have gleaned my information for this memoir from many sources in addition to my personal knowledge of the subject. In particular, I must acknowledge my debt to Lord Castlerosse's racy autobiography which was, unfortunately, never finished and has not been published. Covering a wider range was Leonard Mosley's *Castlerosse*, a thorough and admirable study which can be regarded as the definitive work on the subject. Sonia Keppel's delightful book of reminiscences, *Edwardian Daughter*, provided a fortunate supplement to Lord Castlerosse's own account of his holiday visit in the summer of 1914 to Clingendaal in Holland. For by a happy chance, *Edwardian Daughter* describes the house-party of which Castlerosse was a member until the threat of war broke it up.

Study of 'The Londoner's Log' in the *Sunday Express* over the years proved to be a mine of information about the author as well as being a monument to his achievement in journalism.

The Castlerosse file, which I consulted in the Beaverbrook Library, through the kindness of Mr A. J. P. Taylor, yielded much that was of value.

Naturally, the recollections of relations and friends of Lord Castlerosse in England and Ireland were freely drawn upon. Thus, I must acknowledge with gratitude the help and kindness I received in preparing this book from the late Lord Nugent, Lord de Vesci, Mrs Grosvenor, Sir Max Aitken, Bart, the Hon. Mrs. Kidd, Lady Sybil Rowley, Lady Mary Lygon, Sir Carol Reed, Mr John Gordon, Mr Tom Driberg,

MP, Brigadier Wardell, Mr S. W. Alexander, Mr Percy Hoskins, Mr William Gerhardi, Mr H. L. Conner, and many others. I need not add that for the opinions expressed in the book – and any errors that may have crept into it – they are in no way responsible.

The brilliant caricature of Lord and Lady Castlerosse by Antony Wysard is reproduced on the jacket by kind permission of the artist and Mr Osbert Lancaster, owner of the original. To both of these gentlemen I tender my grateful thanks.

When Mr Wysard's pictures were shown in Walker's Galleries in 1936, Lord Castlerosse wrote a characteristic introduction to the catalogue: ' Your exhibition should be a great success if there is any reciprocity in life, for I know that a great number of your clients have, at one time or another, made an exhibition of themselves . . .'

I must also acknowledge with thanks the permission which the Bibliothèque Nationale in Paris has given me to reproduce the portrait of Jacqueline Forzanne.

G.M.T.

I

No one could forget the first sight of Valentine, Viscount Castlerosse, and I am glad that I saw him at a time when I was still young enough to be delighted by the rarer works of the Creator and when Valentine was in the full opulence of physique, good humour, wit and absurdity.

'There was nobody quite like Castlerosse,' said his best friend many years later. He was speaking with a kind of rueful affection, for by that time Castlerosse had gone, leaving a great void in the life of his friends. It is quite likely that there will never again be anybody like Castlerosse, that extraordinary amalgam of aristocratic presence and innocent rascality. Sir Maurice Baring, who was Castlerosse's uncle, and who loved him dearly, wrote when he heard the news of his death

> The stupid world, a shade more dull and grey,
> Goes rolling on, for Valentine's away.

To see him as I did then, on a mellow, sunlit morning in the early 1930s, was to have a great deal explained about the man, his times and his background, which would have been incomprehensible without that vision. This is what I saw, section by section, as my eyes moved from the floor upwards, for I had been at work at a table nearby and my gaze rose slowly to scan this person who had suddenly come between me and the daylight.

11

The feet were small and were shod in slippers of a Norwegian style which was just then becoming fashionable. What caught my eye about them in particular, however, were the two crossed Cs in white that were embroidered on them. They seemed to me to have a certain panache or a plain vulgarity – at any rate, to be highly individual.

The man above them was large – immense in girth and breadth of shoulders. He must be, I thought – but my imagination shrank from the task of estimating his weight. A few months before, he had turned the scales in Berry's wineshop in St James's Street at 18 stone 3 pounds. Very soon Dr Dengler's Sanatorium at Baden-Baden would be grappling once again with the respectively difficult and impossible tasks of reducing Lord Castlerosse's weight to something more reasonable and persuading him to discipline his appetites.

There was a dazzling expanse of white waistcoat, a black jacket with a flower in the buttonhole which on any other mortal would have been thought excessively large. A Brigade tie. But what caught my eye, above all, was that the crossed Cs of his slippers were repeated, in white, on each of the buttons of his jacket. Thus, I thought, with that final touch of flamboyance, that indulgence in excess, is how a patrician born should, and nobody of lesser rank would dare, dress.

This human landscape, at once impressive and idiosyncratic, culminated in a head, rubicund, fleshy, bald and shining, with blue and slightly protuberant eyes in which two devils of mischief were dancing. The nose was remarkable: long, high-bridged with a decided hook and ending in a sharp point twisted somewhat to one side. The nose of a Roman pro-consul, one would have said, were it not for the fact that just such a nose appears time and again in the streets and bars of Irish towns.

On the other hand, Castlerosse used to refer proudly to his Jewish great-grandmother, a woman endowed with a considerable strength of character. But there were times too when he seemed to forget this matriarch and would insist that his mother's family, the Barings, began with a Lutheran pastor in the Palatinate. In any case, the two claims are not at all incompatible. And, whatever may be said about the evidence of his profile, it is certain that he had inherited only some of the characteristics of his Semitic ancestors.

To sum him up: Valentine had the face and the presence of a Renaissance prince – say, Henry VIII before final sourness overtook him – the over-ripe philosophy of Falstaff and the impudence of W. C. Fields. There was, too, something about his nose which reminded one who saw him of King Edward VII.

Under one arm, he carried a box of cigars, as a priest carries a missal. His bald head shone with the perfumed dressing he used for his hair. One arm, the right, was held out awkwardly at an angle. When he laughed, it shook helplessly in the air. The misfortune of war had cost Valentine an elbow.

The last impression was the same as the first – that of a vast and clumsy body delicately balanced on small and elegant feet. Even if I had heard nothing of the legend which had grown up round the man, I did not need to be told that here before me was a great personality, brilliant and, probably, slightly mad; genial and wayward; the despair of his family and (if he had one) his dietician, a problem to his tailors and his accountants, a plague to his creditors, a gift to caricaturists, the worry of his friends.

Let it be said that no shadow of such a worry clouded his countenance, which belonged, as with all men of his type, to a man utterly at ease with the world and on the best of terms with his bank manager. Yet it is quite likely that at that moment this genial apparition was, in effect, a bankrupt. Never did anyone carry off the part with greater assurance. '*N'avoir que quatre sous et se faire le Grand Condé*' – to have only tuppence in your pocket and act like the first noble in the land. Such was Valentine Browne, Viscount Castlerosse, heir to the earldom of Kenmare.

2

The Brownes came to Ireland in the first year of the reign of Queen Elizabeth. The first of them, Sir Valentine Browne, Bart, was English of the English, and the owner of land in Totteridge, Hertfordshire. He was appointed Surveyor General in 1559, and after spending forty years as a Crown official died and was buried in Dublin. His sons, by that time landed proprietors in the south-west of Ireland, reverted to Catholicism and married into the Irish aristocracy – O'Sullivans, Fitzgeralds of Desmond, MacCarthys, Butlers, O'Briens, Plunketts – and, as their zeal for the old religion was testified anew, so did their bounds grow wider. The family held a fine balance between loyalty to the Faith and the natural desire of proprietors to see an extension of their estates.

There were several devices by which this end could be accomplished. Thus, they had a mortgage on lands belonging to the Earl of Clancarty which, when that Irish nobleman rashly rebelled against the Queen, was converted into a title to these lands. Two fortunate marriages of Kerry Brownes with Limerick Brownes, their cousins, resulted in the union of two big properties into a single estate of great extent and considerable wealth.

Sometime between 1620 and 1630, one of the brightest jewels in the Irish Crown came into their possession. The King gave the Sir Valentine Browne of his day ' the islands, lakes and fisheries of Killarney '. Hardly surprising, then, that Valentine Castlerosse was indignant when he read in the newspaper just three hundred years later that Muckross Estates had given lakes and all to the Irish nation. Muckross Estates was, in Valentine's view, giving away something that did not belong to it.

But during the seventeenth century the conflict between religion and loyalty intervened to complicate this picture of a peaceful, intelligent family of landowners bent, through lucrative marriages and other means, on extending its holdings. The Brownes emerged reasonably intact. The alarming visitation of Oliver Cromwell passed over them and left no more than the legend that Ross Castle, their chief seat, had been the last in the Kingdom to succumb to the assault of the Protector's troops. When, a generation later, the question was whether to fight for James II or William of Orange, the Browne of the hour was, decisively, a Jacobite. This, as it proved, was a miscalculation, although not a fatal one. Browne raised a regiment of foot for his unfortunate monarch and was made Viscount Kenmare in the peerage of Ireland at a moment when James was no longer King of England but was still, theoretically and legally, King of Ireland.

Such considerations became academic when the Jacobite army was beaten at Aughrim and Kenmare was made prisoner. However, the Lord was on the side of the righteous. Kenmare's title might be disputed, but he managed to hold on to most of the family property, or win it back. And, in due course, when the wind in Whitehall blew more favourably to the aristocracy in Ireland, an old name returned to the roll of the Irish nobility. Kenmare became the title of an earldom after 1801.

There were, about this time, many new creations and promotions in the Irish peerage, amid the flurry of coronets occasioned by the union of the Irish and British Parliaments. (In the same way, there had been impressive promotions in the Scottish peerage in 1707, the year of the Anglo-Scottish

Parliamentary Union.) Lord Cornwallis, who acted for the British government in the Irish union negotiations, reported that Kenmare was one of those titles he was 'obliged' to promise in order to carry 'the business' through the Irish Parliament. The Brownes had a considerable political influence at a time when it was a saleable commodity. But politics was one thing and religion another. Kenmare remained staunchly Catholic and faithful to the spiritual rights of the Catholic population.

At the beginning of the nineteenth century, the Brownes were counted among the few British noble families – there were twenty-eight of them – that were possessed of more than 100,000 acres. Totting up their properties one by one, they arrived at the respectable total of 130,000 acres in the counties of Limerick, Kerry and Cork. It was believed, perhaps rightly, that their rent roll of £34,000 (estimate of 1883) was a gross understatement of their real income, although it must be remembered that the great part of the property, in the mountain lands of Kerry, was on unproductive soil.

At this rate, the Kenmare earls were rich enough and certainly grand enough to move from Ross Castle to an agreeable house in Killarney. Then an English Lady Kenmare in the nineteenth century decided that this was not good enough. Her upbringing at Longleat, home of her father, the Marquis of Bath, had given her a standard of magnificence which her Irish house could not match. She wanted to build a new house on the high ground above the town. Finding, conveniently, that the lakeside air was bad for her health, she persuaded her husband to build an imposing. bogus Elizabethan mansion in red brick, which from every window commanded a view of the lake. So, at least, it was said.

The house had innumerable gables and a wealth of fine panelling and elaborate plaster ceilings. In short, it looked, on the outside, like an expensive girls' school and on the inside like an old-fashioned hotel. Wonder of wonders, the doorhandles were made from the backs of enamelled antique watches. This was an item in the décor which particularly impressed visitors and the writers of descriptive handbooks.

The house pleased the Lady Kenmare who had wished it built and who had devoted herself to planning the gardens, which were universally acknowledged to be beautiful. It made less appeal to her descendants, who heard with more chagrin than pride that it had cost a quarter of a million to build. The figure may or may not have been exact but, in an age when the old affluence of the Kenmares was dwindling, it aroused only the wryest of smiles from later generations of the family. It was in this now vanished mansion that the Kenmares entertained Queen Victoria. For by that time they had moved into the royal circle. Valentine's grandfather was Comptroller of the Royal Household and later Lord Chamberlain.

Lord Kenmare was at the same time a highly respected figure in Catholic circles and a director of many companies. He gave lavishly towards the building of Killarney Cathedral, an imposing example of modern Gothic which dominates the little lakeside town. Valentine, when passing the Cathedral, would sigh deeply as if every one of its stones had been torn from his heart. He also claimed that his grandfather impoverished himself by paying off the capital, which numerous investors had subscribed through their confidence in him, in a company that went bankrupt. It seems, indeed, that with this Victorian Lord Kenmare the fortunes of the Brownes reached their peak. Certainly neither Valentine nor his father held such distinguished appointments as he, or were able to make such impressive benefactions.

When Valentine's grandfather died in 1905 and was buried in the family vault in the cathedral, he left £132,000. Thus he had not been ruined by his generosity. His son, Valentine's father, was tall and handsome, a superb horseman who carried off countless prizes at the Dublin Horse Show and was renowned as a dandy. He was, in short, all that an Irish aristocrat was expected to be in that land where, last of all, aristocracy is still resentfully admired. In 1887 he married Elizabeth Baring, the first Lord Revelstoke's daughter.

Valentine Edward Charles, his eldest son, was born on 29 May 1891. He had two elder sisters and was, in due course, followed by two younger brothers. He grew up, as a child should, among the scenes and the people of the family estate. Before many years had passed, his elegant father, superbly mounted, was accompanied on his morning ride by a bright-eyed, red-cheeked little boy on a fat Shetland pony.

The other side of Valentine's family, the Barings, were glamorous in a different way and were certainly more in the public eye than the Brownes. They were an eminent clan of bankers who had among them no fewer than three peerages. Lord Cromer, the great pro-consul who had dragged Egypt out of a morass of bankruptcy and corruption, was the most celebrated of the family. But the Barings had been active and distinguished in the City of London for generations, ever since the first Baring came over from the Continent to seek his fortune in England. Valentine was immensely proud of his Baring blood and aware of their reputation for astuteness in business, although he himself was a living testimony to the frailty of the hereditary principle.

When a film was produced in 1934, based on a history of the House of Rothschild, the Barings were thrown into a state of indignation. The film, they said, showed Baring Brothers as a business of minor importance, bankers who, in a hint of crisis, were glad to run to the Rothschilds for help. The Barings, therefore, sent a protest to the Board of Film Censors. Valentine's Baring blood boiled along with that of his relatives. According to him, when Sir Francis Baring died in 1810, he had left £7,000,000 and was described by Erskine as ' the first merchant in Europe '. After Waterloo, he pointed out, it was the Barings who floated the

French Reparation Loan, with the encouragement of the Duke of Wellington. In this important operation they had the collaboration of Hope of Amsterdam. Rothschilds were not brought into the deal at all because they were not considered big enough or grand enough. That was the Baring view of the historical situation.

Baring's protest against the film seems to have been in vain. The company which made the film said that they had understood Barings had approved the story as it was told in the film. And the Censors, when they were approached, swore that they were under the same misapprehension.

Valentine, when he heard the story, was reminded of Labouchère, father of the famous Radical journalist, who was a clerk in Barings' Amsterdam office. Young Labouchère set his sights high. He wished to marry a Miss Hope and become a partner in the Baring business. Miss Hope's father, the fabulously rich head of the firm, rejected the young man's suit. 'Would it make any difference,' asked Labouchère, ' if I told you I am shortly to become a partner in Barings?' It was obvious that it might. Then he went to Barings, asked for a partnership in the firm, and was rejected. 'Would it make any difference,' he asked, ' if I told you I was shortly to marry Miss Hope?' Thus, said Valentine, he won the girl and the partnership.

The pride of race tugged in two directions in Valentine's blood. The ancient aristocracy of the soil pulled against the fame and brillance of the patricians of finance. He was aware of them both. Yet there could be no doubt which of the two was dominant. Valentine, the West End playboy and distinguished journalist, was first and foremost an Irish nobleman. John Gordon says, ' When Valentine was in Killarney, he was a different being.' There he was a king, with all the glory and the fetters of his role. Elsa Maxwell, who visited Killarney with Valentine and his close friend, Mrs Randolph Hearst, brings her own testimony to support this, as will be seen.

3

One day Valentine was snatched away from his idyllic life among the mountains and the lakes of Kerry. There befell him what happens to other and less fortunate boys: education. After much study and reflection, his parents had decided that their first-born son, whom they suspected of stupidity and, worse, of eccentricity, had better go to a prep school in England. There the atmosphere would be more intellectually bracing than Kerry, and Valentine would have the companionship of others of his own age, if not of his own class – for in the early years of the century the ultimate inheritor of an earldom and vast estates had not many social equals.

The Castlerosses* – or at least Lady Castlerosse, who was the more effective parent of the two – may have thought too that a tendency to arrogance in their son would be corrected in the 'democratic' atmosphere of an English school. What they did not realize was that Valentine had a strong sense of his own inferiority.

In the end the choice fell upon St Anthony's school at Eastbourne. There Valentine was left with the gloomiest of thoughts and there, in a very short time, he fell under the disapproval of the authorities. He was, it appeared, a 'water funk'. This was because he showed some distaste for swimming in the local public baths, the cleanliness of which

* Valentine's father had not yet succeeded to the earldom.

he had reason to distrust. He was accustomed to his own lake in which one did not swim but indulged in a little amateurish fishing from a rowing boat, supervised by an indulgent and watchful fisherman employed by his father.

The truth is that although Valentine had a natural talent for field sports he lacked the temperament of the born angler. Mattie Gleason, who became the Kenmares' fisherman, remembered as an old man some of the tantrums that had punctuated their expeditions together. Screwing his eyes up and laughing shyly, he said, 'No, His Lordship, grand man, had not the patience you need for fishing.' After that, Mattie relapsed into silent chuckles, standing at the door of his little cottage on the edge of the Killarney golf course. By that time, Valentine had been dead for close on thirty years. But his spirit, ample, poetic and absurd, lived on in the scenes of his youth and among the people who had known him best.

At St Anthony's school, Valentine felt lost and unhappy. Yet he was not entirely neglected by the family. This was, indeed, another source of discomfort to him. For one day he was visited by his grandest, wealthiest, most tremendous uncle, his mother's brother, Lord Revelstoke.

Uncle John had been among the counsellors who had advised Lady Castlerosse on the choice of a school. Now he came on a personal tour of inspection. Not only did he arrive at the school in a motorcar which advertised his opulence in the most embarrassing way but he had the thoughtlessness to bring with him two beautiful ladies. As Uncle John was a bachelor, the presence of these powdered and perfumed beauties was unusually hard for young Valentine to explain to envious and ill-mannered school friends.

Lord Revelstoke had been staying with the Duke of Devonshire at Compton Place. Valentine did not know who this magnate was – not even that, in an earlier stage of life, he had kept the famous 'Skittles', the leading English tart of her day. The Duke was not the most brilliant of intellects. Indeed, when another of her admirers, Lord Clanricarde, asked what sort of man his Grace was, Skittles answered tersely, 'More balls than brains, my dear.' But Valentine had not yet reached the age when this anecdote would have made the Duke more interesting or his uncle's visit to the school less harrowing.

When Lord Revelstoke and his ladies departed amid a swirl of satin and a cloud of petrol fumes, Valentine was left, with a new five pound note in his hand, to face the contempt of boys to whom Lord Revelstoke's fame and eminence in the City meant nothing. Already Valentine had no shortage of crosses to bear. For one, his ungainly appearance – feet too small, legs too short, nose too long and aquiline – made him an object of popular disapproval especially as his lamentable appearance was not redeemed by any special proficiency in games or learning. On the contrary, to all that sort of thing Valentine, in those days, turned an indifferent eye. He had not yet found a game in which he could excel.

And it seemed that the effect of education on him was to paralyse his mental faculties altogether. For example, although he could speak French fluently, he made a wretched showing in the French class. It seemed that he was a 'slow developer' – a term which had not yet been invented to comfort disappointed parents.

Poor, miserable offshoot of the Anglo-Irish aristocracy, he lived at St Anthony's for the day when at last term would end and he would board the Irish Mail at Euston. A day later, in the lost green backlands of Southern Ireland, the slow train from Mallow would bring him by way of Rathmore to Headford. Far off to the west he would glimpse, like the vision of a better world, the frail, beautiful outline of the mountains above Killarney. There would be Mangerton Mountain and Purple Mountain and, fainter and further off, the haggard spears of Macgillycuddy's Reeks beyond them.

The lakes would be hidden by folds of the hills until the time came to disclose themselves. Then, visible at that moment only to the boy's memory, came the slow, seaward tilt of the land towards Dingle Bay. At Headford the only reminder of salt water was an occasional gull in the sky. But with that first glimpse at Headford Station life would begin again. Callaghan, sunburnt and friendly, would be waiting to meet him with a trap and he would be at home among his own people and his own country.

Killarney was in those distant days a country of wild hills, of great beauty, of quiet lakes fringed with reeds and bulrushes and teeming with salmon, and of soft-spoken Kerry folk, kindly, devout and respectful to the ruling family. Valentine escaped from the unhappiness of East-bourne, where he was treated as merely another tiresome little schoolboy, to the glories of Killarney, where at every step he was reminded that he was eldest son of the heir apparent to the local throne, on whom one day, the good Lord willing, the leadership of society would fall. It is likely that the boy found none of this in any way extraordinary. He was seeking not luxury and grandeur, but happiness and home.

Home, be it said, consisted not in the splendid, bogus Elizabethan mansion which his grandfather had built at his grandmother's behest but rather in the society of Dea at the lodge with his children Jim, George and Lizzie, of Mattie Gleason at Ross who taught him how to fish – insofar as he ever learned – and Paddy Feore, tall, gaunt, and red-haired, the stud groom who taught him to ride.

These were Valentine's friends more than his parents, who were able to contain their enthusiasm over their eldest son. They found him hard to talk to, hard to understand. The school report, when it came, brought news of talents which might exist but which Valentine obstinately refused to harness. Valentine's mother, puzzled and disappointed, was convinced that the boy was not only lacking in good looks but in brains too. Valentine was inclined to agree with her.

The truth was that the Browne family had decided that Valentine's younger brother, Dermot, was the hope of the line. For looks, for intellect, for powers of leadership, this brilliant boy was outstanding. All the family thought so. And Valentine, in humility but without jealousy, was of the same opinion as his parents and his sisters.

From all these problems and companions there was an easy way of escape. There were glorious days out on the Kerry mountains or on the shores of the Killarney lakes, fishing, stalking, shooting with the keepers. Days during which the dismal thought of St Anthony's could be put away, when in the feudal, flattering, yet oddly egalitarian company of his grandfather's tenants, who would be his one day, the boy could live as happy as a king in his own realm. It was not so small a kingdom either. Men said that it was possible to drive for forty miles from the front door of Kenmare House without leaving Kenmare lands. But the realm would be diminished soon as taxes, death duties and benevolence took their toll.

Of course, the brutal day came when school claimed him again. But St Anthony's did not last for ever.

4

Thinking of a career for their son, Browne's parents picked on the Navy. It was a curious choice, for Valentine had never shown the slightest interest in the sea. But no doubt it was part of some misguided parental scheme to 'make a man of him'. And no doubt Uncle John had a hand in it. One day Valentine was informed that he was going to be a naval cadet if Osborne would have him.

Duly crammed and smartened up, he went to stay with Lord Revelstoke at 3 Carlton House Terrace. From this palatial mansion, which looked out on Carlton Gardens to the north and southwards surveyed the royal splendours of the Mall, he was delivered by electric brougham every morning in time to sit the entrance exam. For these solemn occasions he wore an Eton suit.

He passed reasonably well and found naval life as uncongenial as he had expected it to be. The hammocks in Rodney Dormitory were uncomfortable, the motion of ships at sea disagreeable. The whole sea tradition of Britain was one for which he had no sympathy whatever.

Mercifully, his health broke down. His lungs, it seemed, were affected and he retired once more to Carlton House Terrace where his uncle engaged a day and night nurse to watch over his sister's eldest son. In due course, Valentine recovered and rose from his bed. But by that time he was no longer Valentine Browne. He had become Viscount

Castlerosse. His father was now the Earl of Kenmare. His grandfather had died after a life spent in squandering the family estates on works of ostentatious piety and similar forms of respectable self-indulgence.

Home in Ireland, the new Viscount found a religious task awaiting him. Cardinal Vanutelli, papal legate, was on a mission to Ireland, in the course of which he visited Killarney. Valentine served mass in the Cathedral for His Eminence and, in naval cadet's uniform, was present at the banquet which his father gave in honour of the visitor. In the Cardinal's suite, by way of a compliment to Ireland, were two papal noblemen, the Marquess MacSweeny and the Count MacNutt. Lady Kenmare had a footman named Gilbert; she now recruited another one named Sullivan. Amid the trials of life as an Irish countess and the mother of a wayward son, she kept a sense of humour.

Having decided by this time that the sea was not, after all, a way of life suitable for their son, young Castlerosse's parents sent him in 1905, to Downside, the Roman Catholic school near Bath run by Benedictine monks. It was at that time dominated by Father Wolstan Pearson, in charge of discipline, and Father Leander Ramsay, the headmaster. Father Wolstan was genial and plump, with well-developed buttocks and the nickname 'Bottom'. His appearance reminded Castlerosse of a remark he had once heard on the lips of an Irish horse dealer, 'He kissed you a beautiful goodbye.' Father Leander, on the other hand, was a severe ascetic who had no nickname.

Among such reverend guides and in the less reverend companionship of his schoolfellows, Valentine grew in stature if not in wisdom, acquiring a fair proficiency in cricket and – somewhat to his surprise – an interest in reading. A school-friend named Francis Meynell introduced him to the poems of Francis Thompson, for which Valentine was grateful ever afterwards.

In the holidays he shot with skill and enthusiasm and, one

memorable Christmas, hunted from a house of his father's at Charleville in the country of two famous packs, the Limerick Hounds and the Dunhallow. Years later, he asked Sir Ernest Cassell, a financier even more famous than Lord Revelstoke, whether he had ever enjoyed complete happiness during his life. ' Yes,' said Sir Ernest, after serious thought, ' twice. Each time with the Pytchley Hunt.' That Christmas at Charleville, Valentine was happier than he had ever been before.

The question of his future still caused his mother infinite worry, afflicted as she was with the curse which sometimes accompanies maternal love, anxiety about her son's stability of character. Of course if Valentine, who had showed flashes of intelligence, were to develop the requisite qualities of mind and character, Lord Revelstoke would take him into the bank and all would be well. But try as she might his mother had no great confidence that her son would grow up to be a figure in the City and a pillar of the House of Baring.

Hoping for the best, however, she sent him up to Cambridge where he passed the entrance examination, the Little Go, and won some money at roulette. After this double coup, he prepared for his BA on an income of £300 a year and reasonably elastic credit with the local tradesmen. Eventually his tutor, Mr Lawrence, came to the conclusion that Valentine was not giving enough attention to his studies.

' You are wasting your time here, Lord Castlerosse,' he remarked sternly.

Valentine directed on the don a bland, blue eye of the utmost benevolence.

' Not quite, Mr Lawrence, not quite,' he replied reassuringly.

The reason for his confidence was simple. The day before, he had backed the winner of the Cambridgeshire at satisfactory odds and had given a dinner to his friends. ' I wanted to see more of you fellows,' he said next morning. 'Very soon I was seeing you double.'

The truth is that Valentine did as little work as possible and acquired a taste for gambling and a reputation as a playboy, one who kept two horses and rode with the University drag. One tutor reported harshly, 'His habits are beastly, and manners he has none.' Later Valentine declared, ' I came away from Cambridge poorer financially, morally and intellectually than when I arrived.' It was not entirely a just verdict on his stay at the University.

One new accomplishment he did acquire, when he discovered a natural aptitude for golf. He improved it on various courses within reach of the town.

Meanwhile, his family continued to worry about his future. They scoffed at his notion that he should read for the Bar and dispatched him to a pension in Compiègne to learn French. By good luck there was a pretty little golf course nearby. Another summer Valentine went to Heuter, a small garrison town on the Weser north of Hanover. His purpose was to learn German in the home of Herr Morsch, who had for years been the music master at Eton. Valentine's room overlooked the local parade ground, so that he had ample opportunity to watch the most powerful military machine in the world being tuned up for – for what? Every young man in Germany took for granted what most young men in Britain dismissed as too hideous to be thinkable.

Valentine returned from Germany filled with uneasy premonitions which gradually faded in the frivolous, self-indulgent atmosphere of Society in England and Ireland. As an undergraduate now destined for an Army career, he did a tour of duty with the Irish Guards in the Tower of London and another with the Rifle Brigade at Colchester. During the first, he drilled ' on the square' and had his ankles pecked by the Tower ravens. With the Rifle Brigade, he took part in company training and became fit. With neither did he acquire any deepened conviction that war was at hand,

and that the British Army was about to face its most testing ordeal. Yet it was already 1913.

He played golf from a handicap of scratch, which was in itself a remarkable social asset. One day he found himself drawn in a foursome to partner a handsome Scots officer named Douglas Haig. 'You take charge,' said Haig. "I'll do my best to back you up.' A few months later, Valentine saw his partner again. This time the circumstances were very different. Haig was a divisional commander, on a horse. Castlerosse was a Guards subaltern, trudging along a dusty road in France. It was during the retreat from Mons.

Looking back at himself as he was in those days, Castlerosse saw a shy, idle, and friendless man, without – if golf be excepted – ambition and, it seemed, without intellect. He had great physical strength and a violent temper. His legs were short, his chest enormous and his arms long. It was said that he could fasten his garters without stooping.

Women played no part yet in Valentine's life; he was too shy, too convinced that his looks were hopelessly against him. He was a passionate gambler, and, in his own opinion, a good one. And he was wildly extravagant.

When his twenty-first birthday arrived in the summer of 1912 his parents were too sunk in gloom about their eldest son to celebrate it. Dermot, the second son, was the sole hope of the Brownes. His future would surely be brilliant. Was he not headboy at Downside? If Valentine was hurt by such a sign of parental disapproval, he was not surprised by it and it made no visible mark on his social life. This was as full and carefree as might be expected of one of his age and temperament, the heir to a splendid title and vast estates.

It was true, and the fact was known to many, that much of this land was bog and mountain on which there were more deer than cattle, and scenic beauty is not the same thing as a fat rent-roll. But there was an undeniable magic about the lordship of Killarney and some of it rubbed off on the young man with the imposing presence, the rolling eye and – even at that time – the outrageous tongue. So Valentine was asked out by the fashionable hostesses and at their tables met many of the great figures of the time. Lord Kitchener, for example, confided to him that his idea of magnificence was not the charge of the Seventeenth Lancers at Omdurman nor the Delhi Durbar but the local store at Tralee as he had seen it as a boy decorated for Christmas.

Among his Baring relations, Valentine found congenial company – that of his uncle Maurice Baring, the family man of letters, a Catholic, an expert on Russia and possessing a genius for languages. This may have been part of the family inheritance, since Valentine too was a linguist of note. Through the Barings, who had banking relations with the Tsar's family, he came to be on visiting terms with the Grand Duke Michael and his morganatic wife, Countess Torby, who lived in Kenwood House in Highgate. Through them and through his uncle Maurice, Valentine acquired a gloomy view of the probable future of the Tsarist system.

Nearer home, the political temperature was rising ominously. The British public was dividing on the issue of Irish Home Rule. In London, partisan talk in the clubs and round the dinner tables grew more bitter. The Curragh Incident was only a few months off. Valentine, the most unpolitical of young men, found himself in a strange position. He was an Irishman, of a family that had been Catholic through the ages but was equally loyal to the Crown. Had not an ancestor of his voted for the Union, subject to safeguards for the rights of Catholics? In this dilemma he found that, when in Ulster, where he had many friends, he was an Irish Nationalist, while in the South he tended to be a Loyalist.

In the morning of 1 September 1913, he rose early to go to the stables meaning to ride before breakfast. To his surprise, the ground seemed to be covered with mist, unusual in those parts. A moment later he realized that it was smoke. Kenmare House was on fire through the carelessness of some housemaid who had a lighted candle in her bedroom. Legend reports that the housemaid confessed her responsibility, years afterwards, on her deathbed. The house was burnt to the ground, unregretted by Valentine, who thought it a pretentious structure, an unconvincing pastiche of an English nobleman's seat. It was probably the last country house in Ireland to be *accidentally* burnt down.

It should be added that when ' the Troubles ' came, some years later, Kenmare properties were safe from the fire-raisers. Each time it was suggested that one of them should be put to the flames, a voice would be raised reminding the more impetuous patriots that the Kenmares were Catholics and generous benefactors to the Church. Look at that fine cathedral in Killarney! How much of the money for that came out of his lordship's pocket! The hand of the incendiaries was stayed.

As for Kenmare House, a new more modest and altogether more charming residence rose in its place, the work of Sir Edwin Lutyens, the last English architect with some feeling for the grand manner. By this time there were other things for Valentine to think about, more exciting than ancestral mansions and, very soon, more alarming.

5

As the month of July 1914 went forward on its flowing, sunlit, beguiling way towards catastrophe, Valentine was in Holland as a guest at Clingendaal House, near The Hague, a rambling old Dutch mansion spanning a canal. It had wooden balconies and, at the top, an observatory. There the Hon. Mrs George Keppel was accustomed to entertain a large party of young people and thither she had bidden Valentine, who had passed his Army examinations and was due to join his regiment in October.

The Keppels were by origin Dutch, for their ancestor Count Arnold Joost van Keppel had come over to England with William of Orange. They shared the expenses of the house during the summer months of 1914 with the lady who was its owner during her lifetime, Baroness de Brienen.

This formidable spinster, who looked very like Marie Antoinette, dressed in a vaguely nautical style which suited the house very well. To complete the picture, she wore round her neck a pearl chain to which a whistle was attached. Piercing blasts from this were heard during the day, which were at first startling to the guests and strengthened the illusion that they were on board a ship. The whistle was, in fact, used to summon the Baroness's retinue of Pekinese dogs.

Clingendaal was full of interest for its guests – the Baroness's stables, her stud of Chinchilla rabbits, and the Japanese garden. But the greatest treat of all was of a different kind. It was possible for one who knew his way about the local waterways not only to make the circuit of the house by boat on the canal, but even to punt through a tunnel which led directly under the building. The circumnavigation took an experienced sailor just half an hour. It was a favourite route of young couples in search of seclusion and had only one real hazard, that of being engulfed by a scented cascade of the hostess's bathwater.

Valentine, like other guests from England, was met at the Hook by the Keppel fleet of motorcars after the crossing from Harwich. He travelled in glamorous company. At Clingendaal that summer were Violet, Duchess of Rutland, who had dressed for the crossing in a tinsel turban and a taffeta opera cloak, and Lady de Trafford, equally elegant and more practical in a suit and small plumed toque. There were also the Ponsonbys, the Ilchesters, and the Harcourts – 'Lulu' and his American wife. At the end of the season the latter had left their London house in Brook Street, a gilded mansion decorated in a French style which spiteful critics described as 'Lulu Quinze'. There came too a glittering flock of English beauties and their swains, Harry Cust, Harry Stonor, Charles Lister, Philip Wodehouse and so on.

Once arrived in Clingendaal, Valentine was gladdened by the sight of an enormous Anglo-Dutch breakfast laid out on an immensely long table, covered with oriental china. On the sideboard were old Dutch and English silver coffeepots beside laden silver breakfast dishes. The hour was early but already the two butlers and their footmen were in tailcoats and liveries. All of the staff wore white cotton gloves.

He was allocated his room by his host, Mr Keppel, who was punctilious about those things, although his categories 'Old Men', 'Young Men', 'Ladies', and 'Girls', sometimes got accidentally mixed. The crossing of the North Sea had made Valentine exceptionally ravenous, and he settled down with joy to the devilled kidneys, the chicken and the rest. There opened a period of pleasures – varied, and some more appealing than others. Bathing in the chilly sea at Scheveningen from old-fashioned bathing machines; expeditions to the cheese-making villages of Alkmaar and Gouda; inspections of the picture galleries in Amsterdam and The Hague; a trip to the races. Mr Keppel had spared no effort.

Valentine was among his contemporaries, tall, slim, bronzed young men wearing Brigade ties, white flannel trousers and Household jackets. Like them, he was slim and, if not handsome, aristocratic-looking. He had the commanding aquiline presence which some people attributed to his Baring blood. He had, too, a readiness of wit which does not always go with an aristocratic appearance.

In Clingendaal, brains were present as well as looks. The company included Miss Elizabeth Asquith, doubly charming for her wit and for being daughter of the Prime Minister. Lord Lascelles was there, already a gambler of some note, and the Hon. Ronald Graham Murray, whom Valentine regarded with the respect which a good golfer owes to a man with a scratch handicap at St Andrews.

The host organized outings while the hostess presided over the festivities with the tolerant, almost regal grace of one who had won the heart of a king. Four years before, when Edward vii was dying, Queen Alexandra had led Alice Keppel, the King's mistress, to the monarch's bedside.

On one occasion, Valentine, pursuing romantic adventure where it could be found, took a girl on an evening row along the canal which led under the house. Alas, the rower's bulk betrayed him. For a while, to the lady's alarm and Valentine's annoyance, they were trapped in the tunnel below Clingendaal House. While he tried to free them, there came a rustling noise from above, and a warm, perfumed deluge. Mrs Keppel's bath was over. And thus, to two persons at least, it was proved once more that the Kenmares had been right to withdraw their son from a career in the naval service. But for most of the time the sun shone along the Dutch canals and the gilded young people assembled in the Baroness de Brienen's beautiful garden were naturally inclined towards an optimistic view of their and the world's problems.

But they were, by their family connections, likely to be exceptionally sensitive to what was happening in the diplomatic underworld of Europe and what it portended for the future. Letters came in. Telegrams followed, briefer, more occult and more frightening. Each seemed a little more alarming than the one before. Miss Asquith, as was natural, knew more than the others. Soon it could not be overlooked that an international crisis was gathering.

War? It was not possible. Sir Ernest Cassell, the eminent Anglo-German financier, scoffed at the notion, and for the most cogent of reasons. There was not, he explained, enough money. It seemed an adequate reason for optimism. But the relief which this wise and well-informed opinion brought lasted only a matter of hours. The news was against it. In country after country, reservists were being called to the colours, neglectful of the warnings of financiers.

One day something ominous occurred. Miss Asquith announced that she wished to go back to England to be with her father at such a time. And Lascelles of the Grenadiers said to Castlerosse, still unposted, 'We had better get back.' They left, motored to the coast and, somewhere off the Hook, caught their last glimpse of the peaceful, affluent, complacent Europe in which they had grown up. Of that lost continent they were, with others of their kind, the spoiled sons. The day was hurrying near, although they did not know it, when the prodigals of Europe would pay a bitter price for the easy years.

Back in England, Valentine found that the Army had no immediate need for his services. Accordingly, he went to stay with Captain Marshall Roberts, who had arranged a golf party at Grantham to which he had bidden Sandy Herd and Ted Ray, famous professionals of the period. The day was beautiful. The golf was good. At the ninth hole Valentine drove from the back tee on to the green. It was a superb drive and a feat which, for cogent reasons, he was never to repeat.

After this exploit he found a telegram waiting for him in the clubhouse. It was from his father, who told him to return to London at once.

At eleven o'clock that night a hansom cab dropped Lord Castlerosse at the door of Lord Kenmare's house in Cadogan Square. The streets were emptying and strangely quiet, except for groups of young men, excited and singing. The cab driver said while he was being paid off, ' There's going to be a war. My son will go. My father was wounded in the Crimea. Those were the days.'

Listening to the words, Valentine was aware of a slight tightening round his heart. He was, after all, a young man of imagination. He let himself into the house with his latch-key. A ribbon of light showed under the door of his father's sitting-room. Valentine entered.

' Oh, old boy, there you are,' said Lord Kenmare, erect, handsome, imperturbable, facing the unknown future as an Irish aristocrat should, impeccably dressed for the evening. ' I saw George Morris today. He will take you over with the first lot. It is a comfort to know you will be in a good regiment. In an hour we shall be at war.'

The Irish Guards was perhaps a little better than a *good* regiment, although this would be its first war. But Lord Kenmare was exact in his second remark. War came in the hour.

Lt-Colonel the Hon. George Morris, late of the Rifle Brigade, had not long before been picked by the King to command the Irish Guards. He was a fiery soldier from County Galway with some reputation as a martinet. Valentine knew that he was going to war under the best possible auspices, although he was not sure that Colonel

Morris would take the same sunny view of his newest subaltern.

So it came about that Lord Castlerosse went to war with the First Battalion of the Irish Guards. After a few hurried days which he spent buying a uniform and other warlike necessities he called on his bachelor uncle at Carlton House Terrace. For once, the austere presence melted into humanity. As head of Barings, and a director of the Bank of England, Lord Revelstoke found it possible to lay his hands on forty gold sovereigns, even in those desperate days when banks were shut and sovereigns had vanished for ever. With a comfortable burden of these now fabulous coins in his pocket, Valentine went on to another uncle, less wealthy, who gave him an aged revolver. After that, he made his way to Wellington Barracks and was posted to No. 3 Company of the battalion.

Lord Roberts, on whom shone the glories of victory in South Africa and a VC, spoke a few rousing staccato sentences of farewell to the regiment of which he was colonel. After this solemn event on the parade ground at Wellington Barracks, the battalion was dismissed. Valentine saw his old friend Countess Torby waiting at the barrack gates in a motorcar. She had come to say goodbye and, to his dismay, she was in tears. War, it appeared, was a more serious matter than he had supposed.

'Be back at midnight,' he was told. 'The battalion leaves before dawn.'

'Where shall I sleep?' he asked, looking round him in bewilderment.

'On your bloody arse,' said the adjutant, Lord Desmond FitzGerald, who had graver things to think about than the comfort of a new subaltern.

In that cruel moment Valentine realized that war had begun.

But, being tired and slightly tipsy – for the burden of Lord Revelstoke's sovereigns was, after the events of the evening, perceptibly lighter – he slept on a dusty carpet in Wellington Barracks until at four am the bugle blew reveille.

Valentine rose, rubbed his eyes and set about the novel task of preparing himself for his first campaign. Standing outside the Officers' Mess he was congratulating himself on having at last got his kit on in the correct order and in the right places, as a Guards officer should, when his commanding officer, Colonel Morris, son of Lord Killanin, caught sight of him and demanded peevishly – it was early, and for the month of August, chilly – ' What the hell, Lord Castlerosse, do you think you are trying to do?'

' I'm trying to go to war, sir,' said Valentine, plaintively.

' Then you are the only God-damned officer in this battalion who is,' said the colonel with emphasis.

' Don't worry, sir.' Lieutenant Hickie, the quartermaster, muttered consoling words. ' It's all in a day's work.'

6

That morning the battalion marched to Nine Elms station and Valentine heard – or, later, thought he had heard – Guardsman O'Sullivan playing 'Tipperary' on a penny whistle. It is quite possible that he did hear the tune but it is highly unlikely that he knew the name of the soldier who played it. But O'Sullivan was a good generic name for an Irish guardsman. It still is. At the station there were tearful family farewells. The Kenmares turned out in strength and, to Castlerosse's surprise and embarrassment, wept to see him go.

At Southampton a troopship, the *Novara*, took the battalion abroad. On their way out to the open Channel, came the signal from HMS *Formidable*, lying off Portsmouth, 'Plenty of fighting'. Valentine's fellow officers approved; he himself was not so sure. Above Cowes, he saw the huts at Osborne, where once he had struggled with the rudiments of navigation. On the sea level was Alverstoke, where he had learnt to swim.

At Le Havre next morning, in baking heat, the battalion stood for a long time in a large dockside shed with the sun beating mercilessly on the roof. Then the troops were, rather imprudently, allowed to roam the town for a couple of hours. When the moment of assembly came, three of them were missing, one of them by ill chance a guardsman belonging to Valentine's platoon. Colonel Morris inquired, with some passion, why Viscount Castlerosse did not look after his men better. 'The Irish Guards,' he declared, and apparently with conviction, 'are disgraced.' Valentine was momentarily downcast.

In due course, the battalion reached the rest camp above the town. On the night of 14 August, in the midst of a violent thunderstorm, they set off for the north, first by train, then on foot. To the north, somewhere beyond the storm, the rain and the heat that was soon to return, lay the enemy. But it was some time and many weary kilometres of *pavé* road before the Irish Guards made contact with the Germans.

The reservists, who had been called back only a few days before, found the march a severe strain. At intervals, Valentine, overcome with fatigue, borrowed the battalion doctor's pony, 'Bedsore'. He had by this time won a reputation for eccentricity among his fellow officers, who on this subject were divided into two schools of thought. There were those who thought him an entertaining buffoon and those who were convinced he was merely mad. Lord John Hamilton, an Orangeman from the North, belonged to the latter school. His conviction was strengthened by an incident outside an *estaminet* where two dogs were making love to the interest of the assembled troops. Castlerosse, in his most orotund vein, had commented on the scene, 'I only hope that our disappearance from this world will be arranged in a more dignified fashion than that which Providence has devised for the introduction of life here below.'

After hearing this pronouncement, Lord John hurried to Captain Vesey, who not long before had married Castlerosse's sister, and said gravely, 'That brother-in-law of yours is, without doubt, mad.'

Some thought that the distinction between the two categories of farce and insanity was too fine to be worth making. But, at any rate, having acquired the status of a comic figure, Valentine had become one whose weaknesses must be indulged.

On one point in the march a guardsman in Castlerosse's platoon was accused by a horrified NCO of the grave offence of committing a nuisance in a wood. Brought before the commanding officer, he asked, ' Have I leave to speak, sir?'

' You have,' said Colonel Morris.

' I was not committing a nuisance at all,' explained the guardsman. ' I was only trying myself out, being as I am a martyr to constipation.'

The charge was dismissed.

On 21 August, near La Longueville on the Belgian border, Valentine heard the rumble of guns for the first time. The battalion fixed bayonets. The officers drew their swords. At Quevy-le-Petit, he was gulping down an excellent omelette when the alarm sounded. Hurriedly, and regretfully, he left the dish unfinished. But war is war and it must be said that Valentine, in his roistering way through life, did not leave many meals unfinished.

The Guards, in open order, advanced to the top of a ridge and lay down. At that point, Valentine was ordered to make contact with the Second Battalion of the Grenadier Guards, who were on the left. He threw down his kit and set off on his errand with a drawn sword in his hand and no scabbard. This proved to have been imprudent.

By the time he returned to his starting point the battalion had changed its position, darkness was falling and Valentine had lost his kit and had acquired an impressive thirst. This, at the first opportunity, he quenched with two huge jugfuls of water. An order to move was given, in a direction opposite to that in which they had previously been marching. What was later known as the Retreat from Mons had begun.

But Valentine was not aware that he was taking part in an historic military event. All he knew was that his kit was missing, and he had nothing between him and the fury of the Germans but his sword, naked, flashing, chivalrous but, somehow, belonging to the wrong war. Having, unlike his brother-officers, no scabbard to put it in, Valentine used the sword as a walking stick. It did not seem enough to withstand the might of von Kluck's army as it bore down on Paris.

At Landrecies, some distance further south, he was about to step into a bath in his billet when the alarm sounded. The Germans! It seemed that they had appeared all at once and everywhere. Colonel Morris, a lean man, who knew neither fear nor fatigue, sent Castlerosse to Brigade HQ to act as a messenger. While he watched there in the darkness and with shells dropping, a conference of generals was held. Valentine was horrified to hear one general say, 'Well, there is only one thing for it and that is to sacrifice the Second Coldstream and the First Irish Guards.' At that moment he thought little of the strategic talent of the British High Command. Soon after, a shell hit the building in which the staff conference was being held. 'This is getting serious,' said a general, whereupon the staff talks came to a sudden end.

After that, Castlerosse went sombrely back to his battalion. Faithful to the strategic plan which had been laid down, the Irish Guards advanced towards the Germans and, failing to find any trace of them, turned about and marched in the opposite direction. By this time the men were so exhausted that many of them marched in their sleep. Three guardsmen hung on to the Sam Browne belt of the adjutant, Lord Desmond Fitzgerald, as they reeled along the road.

A day later, at La Fère, Colonel Morris told No. 3 Company that they would be fighting a rearguard action. He added sombrely, 'I don't expect to see any of you alive again.'

However, once more, there was a change of plan. At two o'clock in the morning of 1 September the air was damp and cool, the dew lay heavy on the high ground near Le Murger Farm, five miles west of Soissons and the Irish

Guards, drunk with fatigue after the endless days of marching, prepared for battle.

Valentine and his lieutenant, the Hon. H. R. Alexander,* like him a scion of the Irish aristocracy, sat side by side on a rusty harrow watching an army pass them in the grey dawn. It was a solemn hour, the eve of their first battle, when even the most frivolous young man might be serious and the shyest might speak of what lay deepest in him.

Alexander talked with moving eloquence of the glory of the soldier's privilege to face danger and death in his country's cause. He looked forward with a burning ardour to the ordeal that lay ahead. Valentine listened, deeply impressed, and acquired in those moments an admiration for Alexander that lasted through his life. But he found it harder to emulate his companion's knightly devotion. However, it is possible to put too much emphasis on Valentine's later unmilitary recollections. The truth is that, according to his fellow officers, he behaved with great gallantry during those desperate days.

He noted that, unlike himself, Alexander had lost none of his kit and that he looked, in that emergency as smartly turned out as he had done on the parade ground at Wellington Barracks. Valentine looked with envy at his companion and with small comfort at the sword he himself was carrying. It gleamed impressively in the darkness but he had no great confidence in it as a weapon of defence against the rifles, machine-guns and artillery of the Kaiser's oncoming hordes.

Eventually the sounds of the last column, the rumble of the last wagon faded away into silence to the south. Now in sober truth there was nothing between them and the Germans of von Kluck. A thin rain was falling and Valentine and his comrades ate an uncomfortable breakfast in fields of wet lucerne and stacked corn. In a little, they moved a few miles further south and took up position on the edge of

* Later, Field-Marshal Earl Alexander of Tunis.

the Villers-Cotterets woods. An unseen German battery began spraying them with shrapnel.

'Do you hear that?' asked Colonel Morris. 'They're doing that to frighten you.'

'They succeeded with me hours ago,' one officer remarked in a whisper.

Valentine, who was on the extreme left of the battalion, after a while caught sight of helmeted soldiers in field-grey. The German advance guard. His platoon opened fire and the Germans withdrew over the skyline. Lord Guernsey, a lieutenant and Valentine's senior in the company, suddenly appeared.

'Why haven't you retired your platoon?' he asked.

'Because I wasn't told to,' said Valentine, reasonably enough.

'Don't behave like a bloody fool,' said Lord Guernsey. 'Retire on the road at once.'

When Valentine and his guardsmen reached the road, there was a great deal of rifle fire going on. Men were falling. For Valentine this situation provided an opportunity he had been waiting for. He threw down his sword, still unblooded, and picked up a rifle from a dead man. After that he felt better. He was now equipped for war in the twentieth century. And after all he knew what to do with a rifle as well as most men. Those long, happy shooting parties at Killarney had not been entirely in vain.

At that moment, Colonel Morris and his adjutant rode up. 'Try to get the men back on the south side of the wood,' he shouted, and galloped off to the left of the line, cool, smoking a cigarette in a long white cardboard holder, superbly mounted on a grey horse and very conspicuous. Soon afterwards the Colonel was killed.

By this time the noise of battle was so deafening that Valentine had great difficulty in collecting a score of men and persuading them to retreat through the wood. A machine-gun was stuttering. A wasp flew past his ear and he put up his right hand to ward it off. At that moment, the bullet struck. He collapsed unconscious beside a heap of stones.

When he came to, in considerable pain, he noticed that his arm was lying behind his back at an odd angle. He seemed to have lost the elbow of his right arm and parts of the fore-arm and upper arm. A pool of blood was forming by his side. Strange to say, it was the same shape as the lower lake of Killarney. So, at any rate, he remembered it later on.

A German appeared, looked at him and passed on. More Germans passed. The battle was still raging but by this time was further off, to the south. After a while, the pain from Valentine's arm became intolerable and involuntarily he uttered a cry. A German Red Cross man heard and pulled him roughly to his feet. When a peasant came along with a cart, Castlerosse was pitched into it. He was dropped at a crossroads half a mile away.

Lying there, he watched the German army march past on its way to Paris. A colonel, riding at the head of a battalion, saw in him the occasion for a short discourse on inter-national affairs. 'Do you know,' he asked him heatedly in English, 'that the Duke of Connaught is the Colonel of this regiment? Why do you make war on your cousins?'

It was a difficult question to answer and, in any case, Valentine felt that this was not the moment for a discussion on foreign policy. He was in so much agony that he could not speak.

A few hours and a few German battalions later he was saved from the attention of a sadistic German with a bayonet by the arrival of an apologetic officer wearing the uniform of the Death's Head Hussars. This German rebuked the tormentor and fetched a Red Cross man to look after Valentine. Then he wrote his name in a notebook. 'If ever a German should fall into your hands be kind to him as I have been to you.' The Hussar officer was called von Cramm.

Years afterwards, Valentine made a point of going to

Wimbledon and calling on a German tennis player named von Cramm, who was the nephew of his benefactor.

Morphia took the edge off the pain; two corpses were dragged out of a cart to make room for him. And so Castlerosse arrived at the church at Vivierres where the floor was occupied by wounded men, lying on straw. At eleven o'clock the moon rose and woke up a badly wounded man from Valentine's battalion. In a loud voice he said, 'Comrades, we will say the stations of the Cross.' When it was finished he died.

In all, ninety men who were in the church were dead before morning came. Valentine, who was pretty sure he would be one of them, was by no means reconciled to the idea of death.

Sometime during that frightful night a badly wounded man who lay across his legs, remarked, 'I am after thinking that your death and my death will hardly matter, but they tell me that Colonel Morris has been killed and that will mean terrible destruction to the British Army.'

Valentine could not agree that his own departure was a matter of little moment but he acknowledged that, from the purely military point of view, the death of his commanding officer was a weightier event.

7

Next day, Valentine was moved to a house in the village, where he found some wounded fellow-officers, including Aubrey Herbert and Lord Robert Innes-Kerr, both of his regiment. The latter had already attracted Valentine's attention during the railway journey to Southampton. Valentine noticed he was wearing three tie pins and asked why. 'One can't be too careful,' replied Lord Robert with a thoughtful frown. 'People say this war is going to be serious.'

Now, in captivity, Lord Robert's special quality of temperament shone out clearly.

'Robin Innes-Kerr has been very useful with the Germans,' said Herbert, who, for a good reason, was lying face downwards. 'They think he is a man of great importance. His rudeness has been quite incredible.'

A fortnight later, the sound of the guns became louder again. It seemed to be coming closer. In a little, the incredible happened. German infantry was marching back through the village. Two German medical officers came into the house where Valentine and his companions lay for the purpose of deciding who among the prisoners would march and who could not.

After a brief inspection, 'You will never be much good again,' said one of them to Valentine, adding severely, 'let this be a lesson to you not to fight us.'

Some hours later the village filled up with French cavalry.

A British staff officer arrived. Finding a new target for his ill temper, Lord Robert Innes-Kerr had a violent scene with the local *maire* who, with the inefficiency or bad manners for which foreigners are notorious, could not supply him with a bottle of iced champagne. Captain Shields, the battalion doctor, who had a low opinion of Lord Robert's manners, said that it would have served the Germans right if they had carried him off as a prisoner.

Aubrey Herbert insisted that in messages to England he must be described as 'gravely wounded'. When Castlerosse remonstrated that this would cause a great deal of anxiety to his wife, Herbert pointed out that there were other considerations. He was a politician and, as he had been wounded in the bottom, his constituents would make the most humiliating jokes unless they believed his life was almost despaired of.

In two days a motorcar arrived to take Valentine to the American hospital at Neuilly, which was managed by Mrs W. K. Vanderbilt. The journey was disagreeable, for Castlerosse was very sick, and caused acute discomfort to a French officer who was travelling in the car. 'I implore you, my dear lord, *ne vomissez pas*.' Alas, Castlerosse's stomach betrayed him six times to the ruin of the Frenchman's uniform. Each time he said, '*Quel désastre*.'

For the trip, Valentine was wearing a lady's skirt and cape. On arrival at the hospital, he burst into floods of tears which continued until he was given an injection of heroin.

After a few days, he was put on a train and sent to London in the company of his brother Dermot, who had been wounded while serving with the Coldstream. With them travelled an American diplomatic courier, a large red-faced man named Fred Hoey, who said that he was taking his fiancée's jewels to London.

On the cross-Channel steamer, an elderly lady looked on the two young men with disapproval. 'I hope', she said, 'you have come back to get into uniform.' Fred Hoey rose to the occasion. 'Madam,' he said with icy dignity, 'you have been guilty of the gravest impertinence. Pray go away.'

At Victoria Station the two wounded brothers were met by their parents. It was an emotional scene. But after it was over Valentine discovered to his surprise and annoyance that he would not be staying at home. As a wounded officer, it seemed that his place was in Sister Agnes's Nursing Home in Grosvenor Crescent. He said irritably that he would sooner go back to Paris. But there was no choice.

Sister Agnes Keyser turned out to be a thin, dynamic wizened woman, with a dominant nature, the daughter of a well-to-do member of the London Stock Exchange, Mr Charles Keyser. 'Sister Agnes' as she was called, although she was not a trained nurse, enjoyed a unique position in English life at that time. She was the founder and matron of the King Edward VII Nursing Home for Officers and her friendship with the Royal family had brought her a key to Buckingham Palace Gardens and her own suite of rooms at Balmoral. It was said that she owed these privileges to the care with which she had nursed King Edward when he had come to the throne and was struck down by a serious illness.

What seems certain is that she, quite suddenly, gave up life as a beautiful girl in Society to become the chief of a nursing home and that she gave £8,000 a year of her own money to keep it going. It became known to stricken officers during the First World War as 'a very comfortable annexe of White's'. Convalescent patients were allowed half a bottle of champagne per day, which, according to their means, cost them half a crown or five shillings each.

Of the strength of Sister Agnes's personality, Valentine was soon aware. When the Russian ambassador's wife, Countess Benckendorff, a personage of Olympian presence, called on him one day, she sat on his bed and was about to light a cigarette. At that moment Sister Agnes entered. 'Get off that bed at once,' she rapped. The countess obeyed as if she had received an electric shock.

When he was convalescent, life became more pleasant for Valentine. In the Bachelor's Club in Hamilton Place was a sufficient number of lively young men who, for one good reason or another, were not with the Forces. Valentine found much in the Club to amuse him. For instance, the President was an old gentleman named Mr Gillett, the secretary was Mr Smith. Mr Gillett had some difficulty with the lavatory. Mr Smith used to accompany him.

One day Smith reported, ' I can't find it, Mr Gillett.'

' It can't have disappeared. Look again.'

' I still can't find it.'

' Well, all I can say is that if it's lost, it's your fault. You had it last.'

Mr Gillett nursed a secret sorrow: he thought that he ought to have been knighted, and the loss embittered him. Valentine's first encounter with Mr Gillett was unfortunate. He had been told by a treacherous young friend that the best way to ingratiate himself with the chairman was to praise his safety razor blades. This he did, after all other subjects of conversation had been tried in vain.

' I like your razor blades very much, Mr Gillett,' he said politely.

The old gentleman grew red with anger.

' Young man, you are very rude,' he said. ' I have never used a safety razor in my life.'

Valentine survived this setback and became an habitué of the Club and a student of London club life in general. He came in time to the conclusion that clubs were places where men spent all their time angrily thinking about nothing.

At this time the war was still in the romantic phase, and some of its glamour was shed on Valentine, a badly wounded young officer who had been left for dead, captured by the enemy and, against all the odds, rescued.

Pretty young women sought his company. In particular there was a charming and intelligent young French woman, named Jacqueline Forzanne, blonde, amusing and notorious, of whom he had caught an exciting glimpse at Deauville the year before. Fred Hoey said that she was his fiancée. One day Castlerosse received a note from this beauty, who was recovering from appendicitis in a flat in Portland Place. Would he not call on her? He did, with flowers.

'How is your fiancé, Mr Hoey?' he asked.

'I had no idea we were engaged. His French is so bad!'

Forzanne had the wit which sometimes marks the leaders of her profession and Valentine became the admiring target of her disillusioned wisdom. 'The trouble about being a *cocotte*,' she told him, 'is that you always see the worst side of men, and women you do not see at all.

'French women are by nature faithful and, if the man happens to be rich, it adds a practically unbreakable bond to an imperishable union.

'French men are always faithful to their homes but never to their wives.'

'And French wives?' asked Valentine.

'*Mon cher*, you will not expect me to know the answer to that.'

As was to be expected, Valentine one day asked her to marry him. She said that he would need to obtain the consent of his parents which, being a woman of the world, she knew would not be given. It was not. Lady Kenmare refused even to see Forzanne. Lord Revelstoke, informed by his sister of the incipient scandal, was a thundercloud of rebuke. Forzanne was offered money by the family if she would go back to Paris. She refused with dignity. Then one day Valentine brought her the news that he was engaged to be married – a misadventure which was liable to happen to young men in those whirlwind days.

'Then you must leave at once,' said Forzanne.

'Why on earth?' Valentine asked, very much taken aback.

'Because I cannot abide engaged men,' said Forzanne.

She had some experience in these matters and knew that few things in a woman's life are more tedious than the company of a young man who spends a third of his time praising the absent fiancée, a third being unfaithful to her and a third suffering agonies of guilt over his misconduct. No. An engaged man is not the liveliest of companions for a young woman, although for an older woman, with the wisdom and detachment to enjoy the comedy of love, he can be delightful.

The friendship was, however, only interrupted for a little. Valentine's engagement did not last very long. But the day came when Forzanne decided to go and live in Paris. Whether this was a voluntary decision or one in which the British authorities had some hand cannot be said. In either case the effect on the young and ardent Lord Castlerosse was the same. He wanted to go to Paris too.

As he told the story later, one day it was thought that he was leading altogether too turbulent a life in London for a convalescent. It would be a good idea if he went to Paris, which in wartime conditions was thought to be a quieter capital. Happily, he was able to do so, because a friend of his, F. E. Smith (later the first Lord Birkenhead), who was Attorney-General, wanted to investigate the court-martial situation in the British Army in France and, hearing of Valentine's forlorn condition, offered to take him along.

The expedition proved to be eventful for both men. At Boulogne, the Inspector-General of Communications told Castlerosse that he looked ill and ought to go to bed. Smith went on alone into the war zone when, among other distractions, he visited his old friend Winston Churchill, then commanding a battalion of the Royal Scots Fusiliers in the line.

There were two flaws in this scheme. To visit the line a man required to have a pass, which Smith did not have. And a strong clique among the officers was filled with hatred and contempt for the politicians. Smith was arrested. This led to a first-class scandal into which the Prime Minister himself was drawn. And all this while Valentine was in bed in Boulogne suffering from some ailment, real or imaginary.

His second expedition to Paris occurred at a time when his family's suspicions about Forzanne had been momentarily laid to rest. Valentine settled down in the Ritz Hotel in the Place Vendôme, taking advantage of the special terms it offered to officers, and one day in the Rue de la Paix a taxi drew up from which emerged Forzanne, looking more ravishing than ever, as became one who, by this time, had become the most sought-after beauty in Paris, photographed by all the fashionable photographers, caricatured by Sem. Her portrait was widely displayed on the boulevards. Valentine fell in love with her.

A few days later, he found that his baggage had been removed from the Ritz to her hotel. It was the beginning of a delightful period in his life. The war was near at hand. It was at times audible. It was horrible – and in the company of a beautiful and accomplished young woman, it was easily forgotten.

Forzanne said, 'We will dine at Voisin's. Old Braquesac ate rats in the siege of Paris. He was the lover of Madame de Castellane and he has the best cellar in Paris.' The reasons were impressive, although the last was probably the most convincing.

Voisin's was, at that time, probably the most exclusive restaurant in Paris, still remembering the not-so-distant day, when, as Braquesac reverently recalled, the three *cabinets particuliers* were occupied by three kings. It bore in the anxious Paris of the war the tattered but still gallant flag of a glittering past. And Valentine was just the young man to savour its special chic, especially with a pretty young woman by his side.

On the way to the restaurant, Forzanne said, 'You may call me " *tu* ".'

Emboldened by this encouragement, Valentine kissed her.

'Is it not the custom in England to break a bottle of champagne over a new ship?' she asked.

'Yes. Why?'

'If British ships are as slow as British men they deserve it.'

Voisin's was the only place in Paris at that time where Haut Brion 1875 could still be bought. After dinner they went to the Concert Mayol where Mayol sang with affected gestures.

'Why is he not in the army?' Valentine asked.

'Because he sings certain songs better than anybody else,' said Forzanne, 'and because he has succeeded in being a disgrace to both sexes.'

One day, dining at Larue with Forzanne, Valentine saw the politician Aristide Briand, to whom he had been introduced by F. E. Smith. Briand was devoted to women and obstinately opposed to the idea of marriage. Valentine noticed, however, that he wore a wedding ring on the third finger of his left hand. He asked for an explanation. 'Ah,' said the statesman, 'that was a serious affair . . . It was more. It was wonderful . . . It was youth.'

Valentine spent three months which, later on, he looked back on as the happiest of his life. His parents were paying his expenses, the wound was healing and he loved and was loved. Then, one day, Forzanne was afflicted, as she said, with a pimple on her nose and refused to be seen. Valentine was thrown on his own resources, which in the circumstances proved to be inadequate.

He fell in again with his old crony, F. E. Smith, whom he had met at Maxine Elliott's and who now invited him to luncheon at the Ambassador restaurant. Among the company on that occasion was a Canadian officer whose uniform Castlerosse thought was deplorable. His name was Sir Max Aitken and he was apparently very rich and, in occult ways, very influential. He listened more than he talked and had large observant eyes.

In fact, the two men took to one another at once. Aitken was impressed by the high spirits and good looks of the young Guards officer whose name he confided to his diary as Lord Ross Castle. But it is probable that neither of the two realized that a great friendship was being born. Then, summarily, Valentine was ordered back to London. Powerful influences were at work in the background to bring the idyll with Forzanne to an end.

The homecoming was a sombre business. Lord Revelstoke summoned him to Carlton House Terrace and from the frown on the great banker's brow Valentine knew that he was in disgrace. He was soon told why.

'You have created a scandal in Paris which has been a source of pain and anxiety to your parents. What are you going to do now?'

'I am going this afternoon to the reserve battalion at Warley,' Castlerosse replied.

'The discipline will do you good,' said Lord Revelstoke grimly.

Valentine heard the prediction with little enthusiasm.

His first impressions of Warley were highly unfavourable. It turned out to be a dreary Victorian barracks in Essex, reached by train from Liverpool Street Station. While waiting for the train, Valentine, who was wearing a grey Guards greatcoat, became aware that he had attracted the attention of the public.

'There he goes, the dirty baby-killer,' said somebody.

He had been mistaken for a German officer, one of those 'Huns' who, in contemporary propaganda, were supposed to be massacring infants in Belgium. On his arrival at Warley, Valentine met a young officer who was standing beside his kit.

'Where are you off to?' asked Valentine, amiably.

'To join the battalion in the line, thank God,' came the reply. 'I am sick of this bloody place.'

Valentine was soon sick of it too.

Gone was Paris. Gone were the delightful dinner parties. Gone was Forzanne and love. Squad drill on the barrack square. Route marches along the Essex roads. That became Valentine's life.

It was not a life in which he shone. The technical details of the military art were outside his range of interests. When the officers of the battalion to which he was attached carried out a night-time exercise in the use of the compass, all but Lieutenant Castlerosse returned safely. A search was made and, in the depths of a wood a torchlight was seen flashing – which was against orders. Then came a voice, 'This way, my lord. Mind the branch, my lord.' The signals sergeant was escorting Lord Castlerosse on his way back to base.

It is true that there were occasional trips to London, where a night club run by a lady called Mrs Macfarland was a magnet for carefree and idle young men. She was known to her customers as Lady Macfarland, so that one respectable lady in Society was heard by Castlerosse to say, 'Who is this Lady Macfarland who seems to be having such a big social success? Almost every night she entertains my son John or his friends to dinner.' From Lady Macfarland's establishment, Valentine often returned to Warley on a late train.

Needless to say, Valentine did not easily give up hope of smuggling Forzanne into England past the dragons that guarded the door. At one time he worked out an ingenious scheme for bringing her into the country as a hospital nurse. All in vain. His family and Lord Revelstoke were determined she should not be allowed to enter.

The battle of Loos, fought in 1915, had brought tragedy to the Kenmares. Dermot, Valentine's younger brother, was killed with the Coldstream and Lady Kenmare thought that the light of her life had gone out. Castlerosse, who had always been aware of his own deficiencies – and incapable of amending them – shared the family's admiration for his

Above Valentine as an acolyte (extreme right)

Top A family photograph taken when Valentine (seated front row, extreme right) was a naval cadet. His father, the Earl of Kenmare, is in the back row, standing third from the right

Above After an early-morning supper in a night-club, Castlerosse entertains the ladies

Opposite top left Young Viscount Castlerosse as an officer during the First World War

Opposite top right Jacqueline Forzanne, the beautiful Frenchwoman with whom Castlerosse fell in love

Left Lord Castlerosse by the sea with friends in 1922

Above Lord Castlerosse with Mr Allison and Mr John Gordon of the *Sunday Express* for which he wrote his 'Londoner's Log'

Left The first Lady Castlerosse, Dor Delavigne (right), pictured with her friend Mrs Hoffman in 1930, two years after her marriage with Valentine brother. He felt that he, the ugly duckling, the disappointment of his parents, could never take Dermot's place, especially in his mother's heart. All through his life he felt, with a tinge of resentment, that he was excluded from her love.

Yet this is not at all the impression that has been left on other members of the family. They speak rather of Valentine's ability to twist his mother round his little finger. It is possible, then, that Lady Kenmare, while disapproving of her eldest son and his ways, was susceptible to his charm.

In 1916, Valentine, whose fighting days were done, went back to France as a staff captain under the orders of the general commanding the Fourteenth Corps in the line near Ypres. Now and then he would visit London, the clubs and his other haunts. On one occasion he was walking down St James's Street when a major in some other regiment stopped, failing to grasp the significance of the right arm which Valentine had tucked into his Sam Browne belt. The major thought that it was a splendid chance to be revenged on the haughty Guards. 'In your regiment,' he asked, 'don't you salute field officers?' Castlerosse replied politely, 'If you will hold my cane, my coat and my cigar, I will be delighted to salute you with my left hand.'

At the end of 1917 he accompanied his corps to Italy, where he served until September of the following year. Later on, he claimed that one of his responsibilities in Italy had been to supervise a brothel for the use of the troops. The claim cannot be confirmed, although it is likely enough. But it can be said that Lord Castlerosse had all the qualities – such as tact, good nature and innate understanding of human frailties – requisite for the post.

All this time he had kept in touch with Sir Max Aitken, who had now become Lord Beaverbrook and was Minister of Information. The two men liked one another's company enormously, and Beaverbrook gave him a job in his Ministry. About this time an important party of Baptist ministers came over from America to inspect the British war effort.

Valentine volunteered to escort these Puritan ecclesiastics to the Front. Beaverbrook allowed himself to be persuaded that this might be a good idea.

So the ministers set off for France, flattered by the presence of so aristocratic, gallant and picturesquely wounded a guide. Although it is not certain that the missionaries ever got beyond Paris there is no doubt that the expedition was a great popular success. The ministers loved Paris and became enthusiastic supporters of the Allied cause, although in Lord Beaverbrook's view their visit to the Montmartre front had ruined them as ministers. As for Valentine, he achieved the purpose of his manoeuvre. He was for a time reunited with his beloved Forzanne.

Less enchanted by the outcome of the expedition was Lord Beaverbrook, on whom Lord and Lady Kenmare now descended in alarm, begging him on no account to send their son on another mission to Paris. But soon, with the war over, and the peace conference begun, all hope of sealing Paris and its dangerous pleasures from Valentine had vanished. Infatuated by the lovely *cocotte*, he was squandering money on her and piling up debts with complete irresponsibility.

When the Armistice came, Valentine was in Paris. On the night of universal rejoicing he had a foretaste that the peace might have its macabre side. Walking back to the Meurice, he stumbled over a man crumpled on the kerb. He looked down. The man was dead in a pool of blood. He had been struck by a passing car. A policeman came up and looked down at the body: '*Un clochard* – a tramp.' Valentine went on to his hotel, chilled by what he had seen.

Soon he became aware of something that affected many men of his age: he was profoundly lonely. So many of the men he had grown up with had not come back. Round him there was an enormous emptiness.

Perhaps it fell more severely on Valentine's class than on others. The companions of his youth had provided the officers, not simply of the old Regular Army but of its élite regiments, the units which were most likely to suffer first and longest. At the end of the war, all but one of the officers of the First Irish Guards who went to France with Valentine in 1914 were either killed or wounded. *Noblesse oblige.*

On those who survived the massacre, like Valentine, the immense tragedy left its mark. They returned, many of them, saddened, embittered, deeply disturbed and, sometimes cynical. Above all, lonely. Round the restaurants and dancing floors of this new age, they stared like lost souls. It is not for those of us who have not seen what they did, to wonder at men who shrank back from the gaiety or to blame those other men who plunged in.

Valentine plunged in.

8

The world which Valentine was about to enter was limited by geography and well-defined as a historical period. It was the world of high society which, although it stretched far across the seas, had its capital in the West End of London. The square mile of Mayfair ruled Society as the square mile of the City ruled Finance.

Valentine tried life in both areas and even tried to mix the ethos of one with the other. This, in the end, proved to be fatal. The age which began with the Armistice of 1918 came to an end just twenty years later. Probably, if an exact date for its demise must be given, then the Abdication of 1937 might be chosen.

And what better symbol for the age could be found than the man who, all through it, was its undisputed social leader, the Prince of Wales? He, better than anyone, seemed to embody some of the more conspicuous qualities of the time: gaiety that was not really light-hearted; social concern that sprang from an uneasy conscience rather than any profound conviction; acceptance of the privileges that go with high position or great wealth, coupled with unreadiness to carry the corresponding burden of duty.

Prince Charming, nervously fingering his tie, was the undisputed leader of fashion, as an Heir to the Throne should be. He was the perfect image for the period.

And its characteristic art-form? Surely the foxtrot, danced

to the syncopated music which had been called ragtime and now was being called jazz. The saxophone was coming in, as were white silk stockings for women, to be followed even more daringly by flesh-coloured stockings!

Respectable girls used lipstick; they cut their hair short – bobbed – and then shorter – the Eton crop; smoked cigarettes in restaurants but not in the street. Their manners were freer than their mothers' had been. And their morals? The worst was feared, but the fears were often exaggerated. If the moral reins were slackening, and the social margins were widening, the arrogance of the young aristocracy was as marked as ever. To improve that would need another war.

The social round was governed, as for long it had been, by strict if unwritten laws. Where the leaders of society had disappeared punctually on the eve of 12 August to massacre grouse in the Scottish heather, they now flocked, in obedience to some equally imperative ukase, to Deauville, to Biarritz, to Cannes or to Monte Carlo. And young men who had suddenly found themselves alone in White's Club met their lost companions in the Ritz Bar, Paris.

It is true that beneath the sunlit charm of the Riviera resorts a more disagreeable aspect was beginning to appear. Devotees of the Mediterranean coast began to notice that all was not well with the glamorous littoral where they paid so much for the pleasure of being certain that they would meet nobody in the Carlton, Cannes, whom they had not met a few days before at Claridges.

Irrespective of the danger to the health and hygiene of the bathers, the coastal towns generously and heedlessly donated their effluents, all untreated, to the Middle Sea. There has been nothing like it since Imperial Rome enriched the Tiber by way of the Cloaca Maxima.

One day Noel Coward pulled the chain in his hotel bathroom and said courteously, 'Not farewell but *au revoir*.'

The first skirmishes had occurred in the undeclared war against pollution.

Of the two principal night clubs in London, the Embassy and the Four Hundred, one was formal, the other less so. The first was closely supervised by a dragon called Luigi, who saw to it, with implacable tact, that the unknown visitors, the dubious, the manifestly undesirable, were kept waiting in the limbo behind the band until, at last, they grasped the fact that here was a barrier they could not cross.

One night Lord Alington was entertaining his mother, a stately lady, in the Embassy. There entered Miss Tallulah Bankhead, a leading actress of the day, with a companion. Tallulah and Lord Alington had been close friends. But in the company of his mother, Lord Alington thought it right to put this side of his life aside. He cut Tallulah. It proved to be a mistake.

After being taken by her partner to their table, Tallulah went across to Lord Alington and remarked in a husky but penetrating whisper, 'So you don't recognize me, Lord Alington, with my clothes on.'

Miss Bankhead was a lady who, by one means or another, was easing the hypocritical old London life which Edward VII had been unable to thrust into the twentieth century. If the Prince of Wales was the leader of Society, she was its type-actress, as Michael Arlen was its novelist (with Evelyn Waugh treading on his heels, a fiercer and more serious satirist), Noel Coward its playwright, Epstein its acknowledged, if detested, sculptor, and Lavery its flattering painter.

There were, of course, other night haunts than the Four Hundred, as well known and even more notorious. There was the Kit-Kat. There was the '43' in Gerrard Street, run by Mrs Meyrick, who was raided in 1927, went to prison for six months and was gaoled again in 1928. But her popularity survived these misfortunes. Three of her daughters married into the peerage. Her sons-in-law were Lord Kinnoull, Lord de Clifford and the Earl of Craven. There could hardly have been a more convincing demonstration of the breakdown of social barriers.

It was an age of dotty peers and dissolute baronets, of financiers who rose fast and tumbled faster, of Jimmy White and Clarence Hatry. Some of the rich were very idle, some worked hard – too hard to have the time to use their money sensibly.

The gulf between rich and poor was deeper and wider than it is now but the gulf between them was not yet filled up by a powerful and acquisitive bureaucracy.

Clubs of another kind existed too, the traditional clubs of the West End, more influential and far more numerous than they later became, more socially exclusive and relatively cheaper. Valentine found himself very much at his ease among them : he ate at the Orleans, gambled at the St James's, and held forth of an evening in front of the fire in White's. In all, he was a member of seven of these institutions – in addition, of course, to the Kildare Street Club in Dublin.

Bankrupts who were found out were ostracized by conventional people. But there were no courts before which the mentally and intellectually bankrupt could be tried. They survived and flourished. Violent crime was not so grave an evil as it later became. Life was safer and more orderly. Drug addiction – principally cocaine – was confined to a limited circle in the West End of London. It was hardly a social menace.

Fraud of every kind proliferated. The climate of an age in which religion was flagging seemed to be peculiarly congenial to soothsayers, magicians and charlatans. There were faithhealers like Coué – 'Every day and in every way I am getting better and better ' – and religious exploiters like Aimée Semple Macpherson, 'a red-haired Jezebel who could not make her hips behave ', in the words of an American observer, and who rented but failed to fill the Albert Hall for her Four Square Gospel Alliance.

The Mormon Church sent over a wave of missionaries

who sought converts. Less flamboyant but more persuasive was the Oxford Movement, later known as MRA, which Frank Buchman brought from America to Mayfair.

Society was still distinct from Café Society, but the two were moving closer to one another and the first was looking with interest and even with envy at the second. Young people with looks, wit and audacity could leap social barriers which, only a year or two earlier, would have been insurmountable.

The truth is that the established families, who were sometimes dull, were becoming conscious of the need to be amused. Perhaps, like other classes, they had the uneasy feeling that their position was not so secure as it had been. A generalized uneasiness was, in fact, the dominant quality of the time.

For this there were obvious reasons. An exhausting war had ended in a peace by which the frightened victors imposed severe terms on the vanquished. No sooner had they done so than they realized that Germany was not the only and certainly not the worst danger to a comfortable life in the West. Beyond her lay Russia, tearing herself apart in a revolution which testified not only to the fanaticism of the combatants but also to the unquenchable vitality of the people. How long could civilization last with Germany a vacuum and Russia a cauldron?

Men asked themselves such questions and, unable to think of the answers, plunged back into business – or pleasure.

The Labour Party was rising fast to power, challenging the Tories on one hand and destroying the Liberals (who could, however, be alleged to have destroyed themselves) on the other.

Meanwhile, like priestesses of a dwindling cult, a few old-style political hostesses stood, bejewelled, at the head of their staircases at the appropriate seasons. Their power was not what it had been but their zeal was indomitable – Lady Londonderry was ready to pounce.

Unemployment became a settled feature of the economic scene, although it was some years before it grew into an inky cloud darkening the land. It was a problem which, it seemed, no statesman in any country could solve and for which everybody felt guilty.

But, as often happens, the nagging conscience learns to live with the evil it cannot cure. And while the world waited for Keynes to produce the solution, the unemployed went on suffering with the stoicism of those stricken with an incurable disease.

In Mayfair and the City, in the great hotels and the smart resorts, only a muted echo of this huge and grinding misery was heard. Lord Castlerosse, a big-hearted man with more imagination than most of his kind, probably knew about that other world. But when the time came he did not write about it.

The mysteries of religion might be ceasing to trouble the minds of ordinary people but new and puzzling concepts were coming to undermine the notion that the world was a rational system which could be understood, with a little application, by any person of average intelligence. There was, for instance, the novel pronouncement of Alfred Einstein, a distinguished mathematician, that the universe was 'finite but unbounded', which seemed to be a contradiction in terms. And what was one to make of the alarming speculations of Sigmund Freud, a Viennese psychologist, about the role of the subconscious mind?

It seemed that a flock of disturbing ideas was being unloosed on the world just at the time when men wanted to settle down and put the old familiar life together again after the war.

The age through which Lord Castlerosse moved with consummate ease and ever greater consequence was dimly aware that revolutionary stirrings were about. Few men understood what was happening. Fewer still got beyond the disagreeable suspicion that vast changes were taking place and the solid earth was beginning to shudder under their feet.

The General Strike, the Wall Street Crash, the rise of Hitler, the shadow of another, even greater, war – all these horrors lay in the future, still shapeless but already dimly feared.

Such was the age into which Valentine stepped, unconscious that he was destined to be one of its chroniclers.

9

In the early days of 1919, Valentine was the victim of a solicitous plot to rescue him from Paris. He had hoped that the *Daily Express* might borrow him from the Army as a Paris correspondent but the War Office had absolutely refused to make the loan. Winston Churchill and his secretary Eddie Marsh were brought in on the side of the Kenmare family, whereupon the Ambassador in Paris, Lord Derby, telephoned the War Office to say that he had no need for Valentine's services in Paris.

Behind this intervention, Valentine was sure that he detected the chilly hand of his mother's brother, Lord Revelstoke, whose views on the subject of his nephew were well known: 'The boy is doing no good in Paris, gambling and keeping a woman,' and so on.

Meanwhile Valentine, pulled back to London, was in some emotional distress. 'My Lady' was very ill at the Hotel Castiglione. Apparently, her lungs were affected. He told Beaverbrook, who was then in Paris, that he had sent her £400. It seems – for the language of his letter to Beaverbrook is too emotional to be clear – that he had expected that a bill for that amount would be met. It was not.

Worst of all, Forzanne who, after all, was a woman with some knowledge of the world, had come to suspect that the whole business was a plot of Castlerosse's to get rid of her!

Castlerosse concluded his letter by begging Beaverbrook to visit her and soothe her fears.

Beaverbrook did more than that. He had by this time ceased to be a member of the government. Now he found Castlerosse a job with Lancelot Hugh Smith, who was the inspiring genius in one of the leading stockbroking firms in the City, Rowe and Pitman, brokers for Baring Brothers. Valentine might have done well in the post for which, after all, he had the requisite gifts of personality and social position. But he had too many other interests and too little judgement. His association with the firm did not last long. Lancelot Smith and he quarrelled and, at the same time, Valentine's mountain of debts rose still higher, helped by unsuccessful gambling on the Stock Exchange, by injudicious generosity to women and by the extravagance of Forzanne.

One day he and Smith went down to call on Beaverbrook at Stornoway House. Valentine had been buying stocks on margin, wildly expecting the market to rise. As markets will, it went down. A point was reached where Valentine had to meet obligations of £20,000. 'Now, what do you propose to do?' Smith asked anxiously. Valentine remained calm. 'We shall go and see Lord Beaverbrook,' he said. 'He will provide the money.' Smith and he unfolded the terrible tale of folly to Lord Beaverbrook. Beaverbrook listened with growing horror and broke out furiously.

'Not a penny will you get from me, Valentine. You have had the last. Never, never again will I help you out of your scrapes.'

Valentine was to hear that declaration many times during his life, on many lips and with justified scepticism. Now he listened, penitent and crestfallen. Smith listened, too, but with growing alarm. The two men left Lord Beaverbrook's room together. In the anteroom, Smith said, 'What do we do now?' Valentine, quite unperturbed, said, 'The little beggar was pretty hot in what he said, but never mind, he will pay up.' He was right. Beaverbrook paid next day.

That morning Beaverbrook's son Max caught sight of Valentine outside a fishing tackle shop in St James's Street. He was holding a fishing rod with which he was making practice casts from the kerb. Beside him stood a shop assistant holding a sheaf of rods for Valentine to try. The sun shone, and every care had been cast aside.

But the inevitable end to his career with the stockbroker had only been postponed.

'In all my life,' Valentine confessed later on, 'I have been a martyr to the fact that my competitors worked harder than I.' And so the day came when Lancelot Smith said to Beaverbrook, 'I don't know what to do about Castlerosse. He is idle, flippant, and dissipated. I should dislike very much having him as a partner. But on the other hand, if he were to settle down and take his duties seriously, he could compel me to take him into the firm.'

From this excruciating test, Castlerosse saved Smith by resigning.

Valentine, whose eccentric ideas about costume suitable to a figure in the City (claret-coloured waistcoats) and partiality for sporting company (such as Jack Dempsey, the heavyweight boxing champion of the period) had already aroused the disapproval of Lord Revelstoke, made spasmodic efforts to adjust himself to life as a business man. The efforts grew weaker as time passed.

'It's a disgrace how late you come to the office,' said a colleague. 'Maybe,' said Castlerosse, 'but think how early I go.' Society, that is to say, drink, women, dancing and night clubs, had him in its grip.

The day came when, after a long and sumptuous lunch in the Savoy Restaurant, in the company of Lord Birkenhead, he returned to the City. In his impetuous departure, a parcel of bearer bonds worth £200,000 fell to the floor. They were rescued, but unhappily the rescuer was an employee of Baring Brothers who could be counted on to report such an extraordinary lapse to his chief. In this incident, Valentine had no doubt that he had reached the end of the road as a financier. He behaved with the aplomb that might have been expected of him. When he reached the office, he sought out Lord Revelstoke in his sanctum. Sitting on the corner of the desk, he remarked genially, ' And how is the old bucket-shop today ? '

After this, it was clear to all that Valentine was not destined for a career in high finance. In spite of his Baring ancestry, he lacked the requisite qualities. As time was to show, his gifts lay rather in dissipating money than in gathering it. At about the same time his love affair with the beautiful Forzanne came to an abrupt end.

The final scene between the two lovers was in the best traditions of melodrama. One evening Valentine invited Lord Beaverbrook to supper in a private room in the Savoy. By this time the two men were on the closest terms of friendship. Beaverbrook went to the hotel, aware that something interesting was afoot but not knowing what it was. The first glance informed him. Valentine's cheeks bore the marks of sharp and angry fingernails. Forzanne had attacked him with the weapon a woman uses most effectively. There had been a lover's tiff. Forzanne had come to suspect him of infidelity.

This seems to have been the end of Valentine's first serious love affair. Later, he came to see Forzanne through a mist of sentiment. She became another *Dame aux Camélias*, a *cocotte* who, falling seriously in love with a young man, suffered from his cruelty and unfaithfulness. He reproached himself for his unkind behaviour. Justly ? Or was his remorse part of the role of hard-hearted roué for which he had cast himself ? The one thing that seems to be certain is that Valentine was not hard-hearted. Anything but.

Beaverbrook was hardly surprised by this turn in events. It was not the first time that Valentine had shown his instability as a lover. Not long before, Beaverbrook had gone over to Deauville to see Lloyd George and had taken Valentine with him as a travelling companion. While Beaverbrook engaged in serious political discussion with the former Prime Minister, Valentine did not spend the time in idleness. He had fallen in love with the Baroness de Forest, wife of a rich financier. She was a beautiful, blue-eyed Englishwoman, daughter of an English Catholic peer. And she was married to the ex-Austrian, naturalized British Baron de Forest, who was the adopted son of the immensely wealthy Baron de Hirsch. The Baron was supposed by the newspapers to have an income of £400,000 a year.

Valentine succumbed to the attractions of the Baroness and took up residence in the Baron's house at Le Touquet. But the affair had not lasted very long at the time of Forzanne's assault on his cheeks.

In the final collapse of the Forzanne affair, Beaverbrook once more came to his friend's rescue. Valentine was found a job with a finance house in New York. A year later he was in London again. Even in the more bracing atmosphere of Wall Street, finance was not Valentine's métier.

But there was another reason why Valentine wanted to return to London. Sometime in the course of his agreeable duties as a liaison officer in Paris, he had met a beautiful and wealthy American lady, Mrs Randolph Hearst, wife of the famous newspaper magnate. Millicent Hearst and he saw a good deal of one another. She was very plump and very good-looking, with a large mouth and very white teeth. She had a rich Southern laugh, which came from deep down within her and was particularly responsive to Valentine's absurdities. She had been in her youth an actress in the American theatre, a trouper.

He amused her; perhaps she loved him in a good-natured way from which, it seemed, passion was excluded, although this assertion cannot be made of anyone with complete confidence. What is certain is that Mrs Hearst's husband was, at that time, becoming a close friend of Miss Marion Davies, the film actress. It is quite likely, then, that Mrs Hearst was a lonely woman.

In the opinion of those who knew him best, she was a magnificent episode in Valentine's life, one on which he could look back without regret. She saw Valentine in New York. By that time he was no longer the slim, handsome and romantic young officer in the uniform of the Irish Guards. He had begun the process which was eventually to kill him, and was putting on an inordinate amount of weight.

'He was not so huge as he became later,' said Mrs Hearst, 'but he was already like a great big bouncing elephant. I was almost ashamed the first time he took me walking. He wore a suit with striped pants, spats and a white waistcoat, and he positively flaunted his stomach. He spent hours over his food. And what language he used. Oh, he was very witty, of course.'

How different was the situation when Mrs Hearst and her travelling companion, Elsa Maxwell, went to stay with Valentine at Killarney! 'Elsa was told to keep her voice down. I was counselled to eschew lipstick and powder. We were both to act towards him without too much familiarity. Why, we had to behave ourselves more carefully in front of his servants and tenants than we did in front of the Prince of Wales. Once I tripped over a rabbit-hole and said "Damn". I thought he was going to send me back to rinse my mouth out. That visit taught me something about Valentine.'

About religion, Valentine proved to be equally straitlaced. His two American visitors were expected to get up for prayers every morning at half past seven, which was especially hard on Elsa Maxwell, who was not even a Catholic. But this was not a valid excuse.

'You wicked hag,' shouted Valentine, hammering on her bedroom door, 'if you don't come down, I swear I'll come in and drag you down in your nightgown.'

This would have been quite a task, because Miss Elsa Maxwell must have been almost as heavy as Valentine. But she, the overweight Protestant, duly presented herself in the Kenmare family chapel.

Mrs Hearst, who tried to persuade her husband that her friend Valentine was a journalistic find, succeeded to the point that Hearst offered him a job at £40 a week. But this glittering prospect came to nothing. There was a bigger, nearer and more determined hunter in the jungle – Lord Beaverbrook.

It seemed that Valentine had exhausted the goodwill of his friends and the patience of all likely employers. But if he had reason to feel anxiety about his future he was not a man to show it. And, as it turned out, his nonchalance was well-founded.

Lord Beaverbrook was not only immensely rich, but was a prey to boredom. He wanted lively company, especially when he travelled. He was willing to pay the hotel bills, and Valentine was just the man to travel in circumstances of the greatest luxury and not to complain too loudly when someone else was paying the bill. It is just possible, however, that in Beaverbrook's mind a scheme of the most far-reaching subtlety was maturing. Probably he had detected in his jovial friend Valentine signs of a talent which could be disciplined and used.

Whether this is so or not, the two men were staying in the Hotel de Paris at Monte Carlo on one occasion when Beaverbrook announced that he wished to write an article on Monte Carlo for one of his newspapers. Playfully he said to Castlerosse, 'Why don't you have a go? Look. You sit in one room and write an article on this subject. I'll sit in another room and write on the same theme.'

The idea appealed to Valentine. He wrote. The two articles were compared and Lord Beaverbrook pronounced the verdict, 'Your article is the better.' It was. It was a very good article indeed. Beaverbrook sent it to the *Sunday*

Express, newest and frailest of his brood of newspapers. There it appeared on the following Sunday.

Valentine had found his vocation in life. He was a journalist. Later, he said that only two men in his life had encouraged him, his uncle, Maurice Baring, and Lord Beaverbrook. With all his personal qualities and knowledge of the world he was not cut out to be a financier — that had been amply demonstrated. He was not a farmer, although during a few weeks at Killarney he had tried to persuade himself that he was. But he was, beyond all question, a journalist by natural aptitude and, soon, by training and experience.

10

Not long afterwards, Lord Castlerosse's column, 'The Londoner's Log', had become a regular feature of the *Sunday Express*. It was three thousand words long and occupied half of page two of the newspaper. It was described popularly and erroneously as a gossip column, but it was something more than that. It might contain gossip about others, but it was essentially a self-portrait.

This was Lord Castlerosse as he roamed about the world. An aristocrat, a bon viveur, the escort of pretty women, the confidant of millionaires, the companion of princes of the Blood. His particular parish was the West End of London with its clubs and restaurants, the Orleans and White's, Claridges and the Savoy. As time went on, the scene broadened to include the South of France and American resorts like Palm Beach. At the right time of year, he could be seen emerging from the Carlton at Cannes in a light tussore suit on his way to the golf course. There he was the ideal of that vanished type, the English milord.

The particular appeal of Castlerosse to the public was not that he peddled scandal about the socially conspicuous — he did nothing of that kind; it was not even the flow of philosophic reflections which ran through the feature, not too worldly, not too cynical and not always original. It was that Castlerosse appeared to be living, and was certainly describing, the kind of life which, in their hearts, his readers envied.

His surroundings were usually gorgeous; his companions were glamorous; his champagne, brandy and cigars were of the best. This surely was life as it should be lived, leisurely, sunlit, with not a cloud in the sky, not a bounced cheque in the post. And if there was more than a hint of vulgarity about the writer's absorption in race meetings, casinos and the company of the very rich, this hardly detracted from its appeal. The absorption was so obviously genuine.

'The Londoner's Log' seemed to be the effortless conversation of an agreeable, if talkative, friend. It was in fact, the outcome of intense mental effort, at least in those early years. Valentine often wrote thirty thousand words in order to arrive at the three thousand he needed to fill his space in the newspaper. As time went on, that space expanded. Castlerosse became a national figure. He had, to sustain him, the encouragement, criticism and ideas of Lord Beaverbrook, who had first discerned the journalistic possibilities latent in him.

Valentine, in short, from a wayward and thoroughly unsatisfactory young man, a failure in the City, a playboy in Mayfair, became a laborious craftsman who, over the almost unbroken fifteen years in which he wrote the 'Log', perfected his skill as a writer. The feature became not only a great popular success but also a success with the people Castlerosse was writing about. Mrs Belloc Lowndes reports that in one country home eight copies of the *Sunday Express* were delivered, one for each lady staying there. Thus, none of them had priority over the others in reading the 'Log'.

One enterprising lady went further. She offered to give Mr John Gordon, editor of the *Sunday Express*, a weekend's entertainment with the most alluring amenities, if he would ensure that her photograph appeared in the 'Log'. She was even prepared to give him transport in her Rolls-Royce. To appear in an illustration to the Castlerosse feature had, in some quarters, become a matter of high social distinction. It was true that the ladies who adorned his page included the most beautiful Englishwomen of the period.

Behind Lord Beaverbrook's idea of making Castlerosse the editor of the gossip feature in the *Sunday Express* was perhaps a simple thought which Lord Northcliffe had put into words some years before. Addressing one of his editors he had said, 'Get more names into the paper, the more aristocratic the better. Everyone likes reading about people in better circumstances than his or her own.'

This was a sound, although cynical, view of human nature. There is in most of us an element of snobbery, of envy, of curiosity about those who live or seem to live more glamorous lives than our own. As the generations pass, the objects of our interest may change, the aristocrats may fade, the plutocrats may come in, to be succeeded in their turn by the cinema stars and the 'pop' artists. What is unchanging is that the masses, the public – ourselves – wish to read about those who they imagine are in 'better circumstances' than their own.

So it was not particularly original to pick on one who, like Castlerosse, was twice an aristocrat, since he belonged at once to Debrett and the City, who had the entrée as of right to the highest circles in the land, who was a bon vivant and a gourmet. No. Castlerosse was in that respect a fairly obvious choice.

But where Beaverbrook showed his exceptional insight into character and talent is that he discerned that Castlerosse, the overweight playboy, the Baring 'drop-out', was something more than a gossip-writer, that, in fact, he had a point of view and a personality which made him a social commentator and diarist of some distinction.

For the years between 1926 and the outbreak of the Second World War, 'The Londoner's Log' provides an unsurpassed panorama. A panorama of a small, glittering world – Mayfair, Monte Carlo, Deauville, and so forth!

Quite so. Very limited. But Castlerosse had enough imagination and human sympathy to be aware that his lucky bright little scene was not the whole world. Like so many of the men of his generation, the men of the Great War, he had a conscience. As the years went on it became more sensitive. And journalism itself has a wonderful power to broaden a man's sympathies.

Castlerosse's by-line first appeared on 11 April 1926, although it is probable that he was the inspiring genius behind the 'Log' for some weeks before. He worked very hard during those early days when he was finding himself and his style as a journalist. But to the student what is most striking is the speed with which he altered the feature, imposing his personality on it, his ease of expression and originality of approach.

At an early stage, some of the main Castlerosse themes had already appeared. His interest in money, for example, his fascination with the men who owned it and the unstated feeling never far below the surface that he, Castlerosse, could have a happier time squandering their wealth than any of them. This was probably true.

The first paragraph he wrote under his own name in the newspaper was one in which he shook his head over a wealthy American, Mr Joseph Pulitzer, who 'could make money but never learned to spend it'. It was clear that for Castlerosse few human tragedies could be greater than that one. In a following paragraph headed 'My Day's Regret', he wrote, 'I wish Lord Birkenhead had inherited a fortune. He would have made such a good rich man.'

As a friend of Birkenhead's, Castlerosse spoke with some authority. But there can be little doubt that what was really in his mind was the uses to which he, Lord Castlerosse, would put money if he had it. The thought never failed to excite his imagination.

Another of the themes that were soon to be recognized as Valentine's favourites made an early appearance in the 'Log'

– his interest in gambling and his sympathy with its victims. He told of a French aristocrat, the Marquis de Gouy d'Ary, who lost so much money at the gaming tables that he was forced to retire with his family to live in Florence, where living was cheap. The family went by train, such was their poverty. At a station on the way one of the Marquis's children read the inscription on the side of the coach. ' Papa ', asked the little boy, ' what is *chemin de fer?*' A look of anguish came over the Marquis's face as he explained to his son one of the meanings of this expression. The other meaning, the more tragic one, he left for time to elucidate.

Every now and then Castlerosse would slip into his feature a practical warning to the unwary gambler, such as, ' If I were you, I should not bet with George Morton of 58 Pall Mall for he does not pay.' On that subject, Lord Castlerosse knew what he was talking about.

His exuberant gift of phrase added enormously to the appeal of the ' Log ' which, as time went on, became more easily flowing, delightfully meandering and apparently inconsequential. If a particularly poetic metaphor occurred to him, he usually invented an old Irish chum, an ex-Guardsman or a stablehand, into whose mouth he put the gem.

At Ascot, for example, he met one whom he had known as a chimney sweep in Ireland. The ex-sweep, looking at the Royal Enclosure with disdain, said, ' There are individuals in there whose chimneys I would not even sneeze down.'

' But I thought you were a Socialist?' said Castlerosse.

' And why not?' asked the sweep. ' With my wife being a Conservative?'

On another occasion, Valentine ran into an Irish ex-soldier whom he accused of having taken too much drink. The man was highly indignant. ' I have not had as much, your honour,' he protested, ' as would baptize a fairy.'

One day a thought appeared in the feature which was destined to play an increasing part in Castlerosse's philosophy. ' Marriage,' he decided, ' means a change in people's lives and we are nearly all conservatives at heart.' And later, 'Marriage proves nothing. It is only in divorce that proof is necessary.' But it was clear that the problem was much on his mind, and the final answer had not yet been given.

Up and down the land, thousands of women readers felt that they were reading the early instalments of an exciting serial story. For the happiest, the most comfortably married of women there is no thought so exciting as that an eligible bachelor is near at hand. The next chapter of the story was nearer than anyone could have supposed, least of all Castlerosse who recorded it.

In October, he went to Newmarket to the races. 'How amusing racing would be,' he noted, 'if it were not for the horses. They take people's minds off conversation.' They do worse. They win or lose races in the most inconsiderate manner. On that occasion Castlerosse had been told to back a horse named Nipisiquit and he had failed to do so. It won.

That evening he sat rather disconsolately at dinner in a restaurant with a wise, elderly woman companion.

'You want cheering up,' she said. 'Look at that woman who has just come in.'

Castlerosse did so, and at once experienced a lifting of the heart. The new arrival was blonde, beautiful and exquisitely dressed.

'Apart from anything else,' said his companion, 'it must be fun to afford a dress like that.'

Later, Castlerosse was introduced to the lady, and confided to her how much he had been exhilarated by her appearance. Her name was Miss Doris Delavigne and she was just about to leave for the United States. Castlerosse thought that he might meet Miss Delavigne again. In that, as time was to show, he was right.

As the year 1926 drew to an end he could look back on a great deal of hard work and a real achievement. Every day – or most days – he had gone by taxi from his bachelor's apartment in Brook Street to his office in Shoe Lane. He had shaped a new style in social journalism by an instinctive mixture of personal philosophy and amusing anecdote.

The 'Log' was allotted more space in the paper, until it filled nearly all of one page. Above it, across the whole width of the paper, was a row of photographs, most of them showing beautiful young women, the envy of their sisters. Miss Delavigne's photograph appeared there the week she met Valentine. It was a time of recurring upheavals in politics which, however, made only the faintest impact on the 'Log'. During the General Strike, which occurred in the month of May, Valentine had been much comforted by the fact that there was a steady flow of buying orders at the Stock Exchange. He felt that this was a strong argument against despair.

Then, at the end of the year, with a good conscience, Valentine left for abroad with Lord Beaverbrook.

The first stop the wanderers made was at Cannes, where Castlerosse saw the Casino with the mixture of moral superiority and apprehension suitable to one who had not gambled for four years. He fell in with an American who did not at all approve of his puritanical attitude.

'While Columbus sailed,' he pointed out, 'the crew gambled.'

'I never gamble,' said Castlerosse primly.

'But surely,' said the American, 'as a good Catholic you should remember that the Vatican is the biggest shareholder in the Casino here. Not that the Church actually bought shares in the enterprise. Oh dear no. But a good many Catholics whose prayers have been answered at the tables have left their shares to the Church.'

Impressed as he always was by a mixture of the spiritual and the material, Castlerosse departed for the mountains behind the town where he was invited to shoot wild boar. The expedition was pleasant but did not harm the wild boar. While it lasted, Castlerosse had time to reflect on gambling.

He decided that there were two recipes for fame. If you are a woman, gamble heavily; if you are a man, subscribe to the party funds. The woman will then be endowed with a past, the man with a title.

In a tobacconist's shop in Cannes, he ran into an elderly gentleman of distinguished appearance who bowed politely to him and who reminded him of someone – who was it? Castlerosse asked the man's name. He was told, 'That is M. de Sévérac.' Then he remembered that at home in Killarney there was a portrait of a Comte de Sévérac who had married an ancestress of his long ago. No doubt there was a family likeness. That must be why the man seemed familiar. But upon making further inquiries at the tobacconist's he was told that M. de Sévérac came to the Riviera only in winter. He was a croupier.

'No wonder,' said Castlerosse, 'that I thought I recognized him!'

From Cannes, Castlerosse and his companion went on to Naples, Athens, Damascus and to Jerusalem.

Castlerosse took a particular interest in the Middle East. Had not his mother's uncle been Lord Cromer, the great proconsul of Egypt with whom, it may be said, the modern history of that country begins?

Lord Cromer's mother was one of those women who think that if their children fail to measure up to certain standards which they have arbitrarily chosen, then the young people must be beneath the level at which any serious attention should be paid to them. Lord Cromer's mother may have reminded Castlerosse of his own. She took no interest whatever in the education of her children except that of her eldest son, whom she cynically sent to Eton. The future Lord Cromer went to the local grammar school, after which his mother gave him £100 and sent him out into the world to fend for himself. A few years later, having contrived to make his way in life, he came back and found his mother characteristically reading Plato. He translated a few sentences into English, whereupon his mother said, ' Are you my son, Minor?'

' Yes, mama,' said the boy.

'Then you are not so foolish as I thought, my son,' said the mother, and resumed her reading of philosophy.

After those months' sojourn in the East, Castlerosse returned to London – the London of the gambling clubs, like Captain Walker's (off Piccadilly), the moneylenders, the cheerful rogues like Billy Doyle whom he had known for some years and whose weakness was – as Castlerosse gracefully put it – that he did not leave enough to chance when playing cards.

He returned to the office in Shoe Lane, to the tedious business of attending to his accumulated correspondence and less onerous duties such as selecting the photographs for the top of his feature. He made no secret of the sole criterion that influenced him – ' I have absolutely no excuse for the photograph of Lady Maureen Stanley, except that I insisted on publishing the picture of the prettiest woman I could think of.'

One old thought returned to trouble him with the April winds. ' I am beginning to think,' he confided in his readers, ' that I ought to get married.' The arguments for and against were stated but the issue was not settled one way or the other. ' I live in one room and eat out. This leads to incidents . . . but not to a standardized life. On the other hand, I carry my worries under my hat and nobody seems particularly interested in arranging a marriage for me. I should like,' he decided, ' to marry a good-natured, jolly woman.'

This is a favourite illusion of the male predator in the jungle and it was to haunt Castlerosse through many hopes and experiences.

I I

When he came back to London Castlerosse found that notoriety had befallen him. Already he had appeared as Henry VIII at a fancy dress ball. He had grown a beard for the purpose and had been much admired in the part. Indeed, but for a jovial twinkle in the eye, here to the life was the masterful husband of Katherine of Aragon, Anne Boleyn, etc. He had been seized on by the caricaturists. Now the novelists had moved in.

Michael Arlen, the brilliant Armenian precursor of Coward the playwright and Waugh the novelist, knew Valentine and put him down in a novel. Arnold Bennett, who had apparently observed Castlerosse closely did the same. Arlen's portrait ran as follows:

> Reginald, eleventh Earl of Mount Wyroc, was not generally considered to be a satisfactory representative of the peerage. He was very poor, very independent, very truthful and very fat.
>
> He treated the truth as though it was the Albert Hall, as something ordinary, commonplace, inevitable, which was easier to walk through than round. Ladies could not bear him, but he had some curiously complete friendships with gentlewomen.

The portrait is witty, paradoxical, not very profound but essentially friendly.

In Arnold Bennett's *Lilian*, Castlerosse appears as Lord Markworth, the impoverished elder son of an Irish peer:

> He was tall and broad – something, indeed, in the nature of a giant – with a florid, smooth face; aged perhaps thirty-three. He had a way of pinching his lips together and pursing his lower jaw against his high collar, thus making a false double chin or so; the result was to produce an effect of wise and tolerant good-humour, as of one who knew humanity and who, while prepared for surprises was not going to judge us too harshly.

Bennett then launches into an ecstatic description of Lord Markworth's evening clothes as they were seen by Lilian Shore, a typist. 'The man,' he concludes, 'would have been over-dressed had he not worn his marvellous and costly garments with absolute naturalness and simplicity.'

On the whole, Valentine had reason to be satisfied with both of his appearances in fiction.

One problem that he encountered on his return to London was a complaint from Sir Gerald du Maurier, the actor. Valentine had made it only too clear in one of his weekly articles that he thought du Maurier's talent had been over-estimated by the critics. Du Maurier, for his part, thought that Valentine's remarks were 'vulgar'. Castlerosse took comfort from a remark of Ruskin's – 'The higher a man stands, the more the word "vulgar" becomes unintelligible to him.' And he remembered what his old friend, Sem, the Paris caricaturist, had said when he heard that Castlerosse was taking up journalism: 'You will find that men and women will be horrified if you leave them out and shocked if you put them in.'

He returned with a keen enjoyment to the life of the London clubs and their eccentric habitués. Lord Cathcart, for example, who sat in the Bachelor's Club for ten hours a day and then in Hyde Park for two. And what if it was a wet day? In that case, his lordship sat in the Club for twelve hours.

Castlerosse once found himself sitting in one of his seven clubs next to an old man of exceptional brilliance who, on that day, was looking unusually introspective. Castlerosse asked if he was feeling unwell. 'No,' said the old man. 'But I am trying to come to a decision. You see, yesterday was my eightieth birthday and it is time I made up my mind about the divinity of Christ.' Castlerosse had the politeness not to speak the words which had come into his mind: that his old companion had better make up his mind quickly or he would have it made up for him.

Clubs entertained him vastly as stages on which the English temperament at its most extreme could be observed in action. Once a counsellor of a foreign embassy joined the St James's. When he entered the club for the first time, the following spectacle met his eyes:

1 An old member had the habit of cocking a snook at anyone he did not like from behind his newspaper. The new member caught him doing it.
2 Lord Clanricarde, an enormously rich Irish peer, ate one cutlet and, wrapping the other one up, put it in his pocket.
3 A member with a tongue like a lizard began to lick his nose with it.

After that, the foreign diplomat decided that he had had enough of English clubs. He resigned.

At the end of the year, Castlerosse went in search of fresh material beyond the Atlantic.

On New Year's Day, 1928, he was on the ex-German liner, *Vaterland*, now renamed *Leviathan*, on his way to New York. One of his fellow-passengers was De Valera, hoping to raise money to finance a newspaper. Castlerosse noticed his habit of constantly looking over one shoulder. Was Dev looking for the ghost of Michael Collins? he wondered. It was a typically Irish thought.

Valentine fell a willing victim to the charm of a fellow-passenger whose company was so engaging that he thought the man must be a travelling cardsharper. He turned out to be the American Ambassador to Spain.

New York, exciting and bewildering, in the grip of a vast wealth and of Prohibition, inspired some of his best writing. ' Luxury,' he said, ' the malignant child of wealth, reigns in every apartment home.' With the fate of Ancient Rome in his mind, he indulged in some philosophical speculations. When this prodigious infant reached maturity, would she turn into a matricide? He was none too hopeful about the future of the United States.

After midnight Mass in St Patrick's Cathedral, where he endured ' the mild heat of holy oratory ', he went to the Tombs prison and viewed, shuddering somewhat, the drug addicts and the murderers in their cages. ' Another pill, another pill,' begged one unfortunate, hopelessly hooked. Castlerosse was having a preview of an evil which, since his time, has crossed the Atlantic.

He inspected the electric chair, heard the story of Jacob Ellerman, a man of beautiful manners who had murdered twenty-three women. When he was being strapped to the chair, the chaplain asked if he had any wish. ' Yes,' said Ellerman, ' I should like to offer my seat to a lady.'

In New York, he reported, the skirts were shorter and the drinks longer than in London. The New York *Daily News* reported that more Americans had died as a result of Prohibition (64,000) than had been killed in the Great War. In Wall Street, far-sighted men were predicting that a crash of unprecedented proportions was about to engulf the economy. These prophets of doom were only too correct. The Great Slump was less than two years away.

Wall Street made Castlerosse think of his own wasted opportunities in the City of London. But he had put away the hopes – if not the temptations – of making money. Although not without many a backward glance of regret.

He thought that he would probably not have made money for himself but he was confident that he would have made it for others. It was, on the face of it, a strange belief. All the same, the City had a lure. 'Even the most unworldly,' he said, ' are interested in women, cash and crime.' And nobody could call Castlerosse unwordly.

An American named Jim Hill, son of a famous American railway magnate, told him how once it had been his misfortune to drive into A. J. Balfour, formerly a Conservative Prime Minister, on the golf course at Cannes. Balfour listened to his apologies and said, ' Come and see me at six this evening.' The young man went, quaking in the expectation of a renewed wigging.

'Pray sit down,' said Balfour. ' If you have a few minutes to spare, tell me the story of the Great Northern Railroad.' But it turned out that Balfour, the languid, philosopher-politician, knew more about the fortunes of that railroad than Hill did. How unexpected the great could be !

Musing on this question, Castlerosse recalled how Lord Rosebery, an ex-Prime Minister, had been asked to give counsel to Balfour when the latter first took office. Balfour awaited intently for the wise advice he was about to receive. In time, the oracle spoke. 'Never forget,' said Rosebery gravely, ' never forget that the garden belongs to Number Ten and has nothing to do with Number Eleven.'

Meanwhile Castlerosse's thoughts had returned to one of its favourite themes, marriage. Perhaps the spring air of 1928 was particularly favourable to this subject. 'Forswear women for horses,' advised Leo Ralli, one of his cronies at the Bachelor's Club. ' They are much more satisfactory, unless, of course, you are foolish enough to bet on them.'

Valentine thought that the advice was repellently cynical. But he was, at that time, in a highly sensitive state. He was putting on weight at an alarming speed and – which was worse – women were inclined to make fun of his figure. He took up riding once more and was in the Row at eight o'clock every morning. 'The secret of life is liver,' he told his readers. He heard a spectator remark on seeing him struggle on to the saddle, 'Blimey, the joint's too big for the plate.'

There was a fashionable belief at that time that marriages go in cycles of seven years. Human beings are completely different at the end of seven years and the change is seldom for the better. Valentine found himself of the opinion of Schopenhauer, who had said of the human race, 'We are unhappy married and, unmarried, we are unhappy . . . We are unhappy.'

At a fashionable wedding he brooded over the problem of why people crowd to see two people being married. The train of thought led him to a conclusion which he found more agreeable. 'However,' he confided in his readers, 'we can all rejoice that executions are now held in private.'

In the spring, London had a state visit of the King of Afghanistan. Valentine saw the passing of the royal procession. That evening, in the club, an expert held forth on the prevalence of smallpox in Afghanistan, but for which, he asserted, the population would soon surpass the country's power to support it.

On retiring that evening, Valentine saw that he had a rash on one leg. He consulted Quain's Dictionary of Medicine on the subject of smallpox and was horrified to read that the most infallible sign of the disease was 'the characterizing eruption which is especially likely to appear on the exterior surfaces of the arms and legs'. Thoroughly alarmed, he fished out a thermometer and found that his temperature was 37°. It was a French thermometer, measuring in Réaumur degrees. To convert to a Fahrenheit scale was a task beyond him, so he sent his servant out to buy an English thermometer. Unfortunately the column of mercury was too narrow for him to see it.

He telephoned a doctor friend and in the meantime felt his pulse. He had none! When the doctor arrived he was notably unsympathetic to the account of his symptoms. 'Eat less,' he said. 'Drink less, smoke less, work harder. As for these spots on your leg, you have fallen in with a flea in the crowd while watching the King of Afghanistan.'

In 1925, Castlerosse was challenged to a duel by M. Hannibal de Mesa, a Cuban millionaire who had, not long before, won 1,600,000 francs (£28,000) playing baccarat at Deauville. Mrs Reggie Fellowes led his friends in urging Valentine to fight, for nobody is so belligerently sensitive on the matter of honour as the friends of a peaceful man. One of them, General de Crespigny, an experienced duellist, offered to be his second. But, in the crisis, Castlerosse did not lose his head. He investigated the record of his antagonist and decided that honour could not be the sole consideration in the matter. 'I have just heard news that makes my encounter quite impossible,' he announced. 'That man has already killed one adversary. I have no intention of improving his game book.' The quarrel with de Mesa was amicably composed. For once, commonsense had prevailed.

Valentine's remark may have been an echo of something he had heard not long before from Mr Ralph Nevill, who wrote his gossipy Chronicles in the card room of the St James's Club. Mr Ralph Fane had gone to France to fight a duel. Both he and his second stuttered badly. On the boat crossing the Channel, Fane had a sudden thought, 'Wh-wh-where are the cartridges?' he asked.

'I-I-I have five hundred in my cabin,' said the second.

'My f-f-friend, we are not going pheasant shooting.'

As the question of marriage and its pitfalls had now become an obsession with Valentine, he devoted the greater part of one of his Sunday sermons to giving advice to an imaginary young woman on how to secure a husband. Assuming that the girl was not over-endowed with brains or beauty, he begged her not to be discouraged on that account.

'Your prime asset is the weakness of men. Flatter them. Study their ambitions. Do not distress them by telling disagreeable truth. Avoid like the plague a reputation for being too clever.

'Do not talk about money. Avoid gamblers – I am the only man of my acquaintance who has given up that vice. Remember that good men love being thought wicked. Stockbrokers are a riotous company. Lloyd's underwriters are much steadier.'

On the cognate subject of jealousy, he had some sound advice to give : 'Were I a husband or a wife who was faced with a rival, I should never indulge in scenes of abuse . . . On the contrary, I should sing my rival's praises night and day . . . Alternatively, I should be a little Johnny-don't-care.'

It was wise, if it was not profound. But the time was at hand when it would be seen whether Valentine could live up to his own high principles.

On 20 May 1928, readers of 'The Londoner's Log' were treated to an article of a somewhat unconventional kind. It purported to be a discussion of life, and especially the relations of men and women, between Castlerosse and a lady whom he called Doreen, although, as he said, she was not Irish. Interspersed with Doreen's observations were thoughts which plainly belonged to Castlerosse.

It was impossible for the reader to be sure where the reporting of this conversation passed into fiction. It seems that Castlerosse was responsible for most of the dialogues – his turn of phrase is unmistakable. Yet Doreen's portrait is drawn in firm lines; it is rather a brilliant portrait. 'Eighty per cent of what Doreen says is true,' says Castlerosse. 'The remaining twenty is illuminating embroidery.'

Doreen confesses that her experience of love has been a bitter one. The embrace of man is too closely allied to the kiss of Judas. This is significant because the lady he had met at Newmarket two years before, the lady who was called Doris, had been bitterly disappointed in love.

It seems very likely that the Doreen of Castlerosse's article is a semi-portrait of the Doris who was very much in his mind at that time. Doreen had some sound practical advice to give to her daughter – but she did not have a daughter – on the sort of man she should marry. 'Marry the greatest man in the world, even if nobody but you thinks so. Faith may not move mountains but it has a wonderfully steadying effect on husbands. Never bore him and always greet him joyfully.'

At this moment in the dialogue, Castlerosse interposed some counsel of his own. 'When you come down to breakfast, remain silent but be perfectly dressed. Put your husband's comfort ahead of your own' – and he recalled how Disraeli's wife was always waiting in the carriage with sandwiches when there was a late debate in the House.

He warned the imaginary girl against exceptionally high-spirited men. 'A sad disillusionment may await her. Beware when you marry a clown that the black vulture of despair is not fluttering in his wake.'

This thought was frequently in Valentine's mind. It was, surely, a shaft of genuine self-revelation, or self-dramatization. One of Castlerosse's favourite parts in life was that of the comedian whose heart was breaking while the audience shook with laughter at his jokes. He wore his heart on his sleeve as a gesture of cynical bravado rather than sentiment.

At the end of the reported conversation, he asked Doreen if she would go through her unhappy love experience again. Her answer was not in doubt: Yes, she would.

The article in 'The Londoner's Log' may be regarded as a prelude to a new chapter in Castlerosse's life which opened just at that time.

In the meantime he sought advice from the sages. On the whole, he found they were against marriage. Talleyrand had asked, 'My friend, if I were to marry where should I spend my evenings?' Valentine's old friend, Countess Torby, assured him that discontented wives were usually the victims of love matches.

On the other hand there was no doubt that love played a powerful, even a disproportionate, part in human life and actions. For the most absurd of reasons. Valentine found himself compelled to think so just about this time. It appeared that some unknown person had borrowed his name to write passionate love letters to a girl whose aunt wrote to Castlerosse inquiring how soon the marriage ceremony could be expected. Valentine put a private detective on the trail of the deceiver, who turned out to be a Mr Murray of a Highland regiment. When Valentine asked him why he had come to do so foolish a thing, Mr Murray replied, with a smile of apology, 'Romance, my lord, romance.'

'Romance.' Valentine took a more worldly view. 'My advice to those about to marry,' Castlerosse told his readers, 'is, Do. After all, they may change the divorce laws.' On the other hand, 'Marriage is a great institution but we don't all wish to spend our lives in institutions.'

So it seemed that the verdict remained doubtful. But, in fact, the decision had been taken. Valentine was at a turning-point in his life.

12

About half past ten one evening in May 1928, Lord Castlerosse called on Lady Victor Paget, who noticed that he was looking self-conscious and rather shamefaced. She soon discovered why. 'Doris Delavigne and I have been married,' he said. Lady Victor uttered the usual congratulations, which were more than usually insincere on this occasion since she, along with the rest of Valentine's friends, had for some time been advising him not to make this marriage. Doris's friends had been giving her advice in the same tenor.

'Will you tell him?' asked Valentine. Lady Victor knew at once what he meant. Would she break the news to Lord Beaverbrook? She picked up the telephone at once.

'I've got your boy here,' she said to Lord Beaverbrook. 'He has just got married to Doris. Will you speak to him?'

'No,' said Beaverbrook, and put down the telephone. A second later he rang up John Gordon, the editor of the *Sunday Express*.

'I hear that Valentine has married Doris,' he said.

'Yes,' said Gordon, 'indeed it is so. I believe they married in a registry office in Shepherd's Bush.'

'Get hold of him,' said Beaverbrook.

'It's too late,' Gordon replied.

The marriage had in fact taken place in Hammersmith Registry office on 15 May.

'The terrible thing is done,' said Lady Kenmare.

Doris Delavigne had already travelled a long way on a difficult road.

She was born in 1900 in Streatham, her father's name being Edward de le Vingne. He was a member of an old family of the Belgian nobility and came to London as a boy of eighteen. He had married an English woman and eventually settled in Beckenham, where the family lived in a delightful old eighteenth-century house.

Doris was the eldest of the four children and grew up to be tall, blonde, beautiful and accomplished. At one stage in her life she decided to change the spelling of her name to Delavigne, the original form being meaningless, as she said. It was not her only assertion of a spirit of independence.

Her parents, who kept a close watch on their children's welfare, forbade Doris to smoke and sat up to a late hour – sometimes until two o'clock in the morning – to make sure that she returned safely from a party. It was an age in which parents carried out their duties of supervision conscientiously, if unavailingly.

Endowed by nature with exceptional good looks and intelligence, well-educated, a talented musician, precociously self-reliant, Doris thought that there might be scope for her abilities at the end of the train journey from Beckenham to Charing Cross. And, as it turned out, the assessment she made with her shrewd, blue eyes was not inaccurate.

She first found work in what is called the 'rag trade'. As she put it, she was selling second-hand clothes to chorus girls. What this meant was that she was working for a London fashion house selling clothes which could be discarded and sold to actresses as worn stock. Among other things, she became the owner of Louis, a *coiffeur*'s business in the Champs Elysées in Paris. Through this she bought a great deal of clothes, which the business paid for.

In the course of her business, Doris met a young actress called Gertrude Lawrence. The two girls took a liking for one another, having perhaps recognized that they had something in common. Could it be called a philosophy? Very soon Gertrude was a frequent guest at tennis parties in the rambling old garden of the de le Vinge house at Beckenham. One day she said to Doris, ' I am going to be the most celebrated actress in London.' To this Doris retorted, ' I am going to marry a Lord.'

The two girls, alike adventurous and ambitious, came to share a flat in Park Lane. This was perhaps an inevitable development. Doris and her handsome brother Dudley flitted over the waters of Mayfair, like two brilliant winged creatures, exciting the admiration of spectators like Beverley Nichols.

Doris was warm-hearted and amusing, generous and – when she had money – fantastically extravagant. After a dinner party one winter night, she noticed that the young man who later became Duke of Bedford was not wearing an overcoat. The truth was that his eccentric father kept him short of money so that he could not afford to buy one. Doris gave him a lift home and asked about the coat. The young man said he had left it behind.

' You haven't got an overcoat, have you?' she asked. He admitted it. Doris scribbled a note on her card. ' You go tomorrow to this address, buy an overcoat and put it on my account.'

Victor Stiebel, the dress designer, called her the ' enchantress of the Thirties ', above whose ' pointed and beautifully painted face was a jester's cap of pure gold hair '. He tells how, one day, Doris came into his shop.

' I like your shoes,' said Stiebel.

' Thank God,' said Doris. ' I'm just back from Italy and I've bought two hundred and fifty pairs of the damned things. Idiotic to wear shoes more than three or four times.'

She had a small gap between her front teeth, but ' wouldn't

have them changed for anything, darling – shows I'm lucky and sexy – and how!' She was known as 'Mrs Goldsmith and Silversmith' and, touching forehead, breast and collar-bones, she would recite the magic spell, 'Tiara, brooch, clip, clip.' Rosa Lewis, who kept the Cavendish Hotel in Jermyn Street said of her once, 'Young Doris may go far on those legs of hers, but mark my words, she doesn't know how to make a man comfortable.'

The question was eventually put to the test. In the mean-time, as lively, pretty young women do, Doris moved up-wards on the social ladder.

One Christmas, when she was staying at Madresfield, Lord Beauchamp's house near Malvern, Lord Dudley arrived to announce that he had just had an indoor swimming pool installed at Himley Hall. Would they all come over and swim? Doris sent her chauffeur up to London with the car so that her maid should pack six swim suits for the inaugura-tion party.

By that time she could afford exploits of that kind. For she was the sort of woman who made an irresistible appeal to men, and women too. She was, in particular, enormously popular among girls in 'Society' (as it was called), who liked her open-handed ways and found her salty conversation very much to their taste. Doris was not a prey to any of the conventional inhibitions.

She had, however, one conversational attribute which was rare among the young women of that set: she did not gossip maliciously about other people, especially about other women. In a society in which disloyalty in talk was regarded as a very unimportant failing – if not, indeed, as a social asset – she was noted for her loyalty. Men were, however, liable to be excluded from the operation of this virtue, as her husband was soon to discover.

By the time Valentine saw her for the first time, she was living in a little house at 6 Deanery Street in Mayfair. She had a maid, named Swayne, a Rolls-Royce and a chauffeur.

Every evening, without fail, a devoted expert named Martin would arrive to dress her hair for the night.

Once she had been in love, madly in love, with a man. She had been bitterly disappointed. Her lover, a wealthy young American who visited England every year for the polo season, became enamoured of a young woman who had beauty to match Doris's and, in addition, advantages Doris could not equal. She was immensely rich and was on the margin of Royalty itself. So Doris was ruthlessly discarded, a traumatic and, it may be, critical experience.

For not only had she been in love with this man, he was, as it turned out, the love of her life. She had the strength and wit to overcome the disaster. But it made a lasting change in her character.

When Doris's path crossed Valentine's, it seemed that she had settled for something less than a romance. Her life, after the shipwreck of her love affair, had been a harsh and cynical business, in which there was more glamour than happiness.

Once, at the zenith of her fortunes, she was lunching with Phyllis, Vicomtesse de Janzé, in Quaglino's when suddenly she bowed her head and, looking up, said savagely, ' You may think it fun to make love but if you had to make love to dirty old men as I do, you would think again.'

The ruby necklace she wore, the Rolls-Royce and the house in Deanery Street had all to be paid for. And the terms of the payments were sometimes hard. In fact, underneath the smart, glittering surface of her life, Doris Delavigne hid something a good deal sadder, the existence of which she rarely betrayed – bruised hopes and blighted sensibilities.

Valentine was one of the few mortals who suspected it was there. He was, however, not the only one. At the time he married Doris, she was sought by another man of title, the Earl of Northesk.

As Valentine knew it would, his marriage came as a shock

to Beaverbrook, who was deeply fond of him and well aware of his weaknesses. Beaverbrook had hoped to save him from a marriage which, as he instinctively knew, could only bring a chain of miseries to both parties. He had failed to prevent it. Commonsense had been defied. His annoyance with Valentine was extreme.

And, in the opinion of those who were best able to judge, he never really accepted the marriage. Thanks to his moral – and financial – ascendancy over Valentine, he had the power to make the bridegroom's position humiliating, if not intolerable. Doris's view was that he used that power.

Meanwhile the news of the marriage reached a wider public.

The *Daily Mail* said, 'The announcement of the secret marriage of Lord Castlerosse and Miss Doris Delavigne has come as a great surprise to the West End, for Lord Castlerosse has publicly outlined on several occasions the advantages of remaining a bachelor . . . Miss Delavigne is tall, fair and pretty with a wistfully cynical smile and a very quick brain. Mr Michael Arlen thought that she would become a leading hostess in London if she ever married.' And now, not only had the beautiful Miss Delavigne married but she had married a title. In the normal course of events, and provided no untoward incident occurred, she would one day be a countess.

When Doris Delavigne's wistfully cynical smile became that of Lady Castlerosse, she did in fact become one of London's most sought-after hostesses. In her charming little house in Deanery Street could be seen millionaires and sprigs of the aristocracy, and young women belonging to ancient families, who were either above the petty restrictions of society or who had defied their mothers' ban on the house.

From time to time there was even a royal Duke to be seen there, although he was likely to be given a paternal wigging next morning when, as everything like that did, the news was carried to the ears of His Majesty himself. For the truth is that the witty, pretty, hospitable Lady Castlerosse was looked on with black disapproval by parents with susceptible sons, or daughters who might be led from the stricter paths.

It was, perhaps, a small price to pay for having achieved, by various means and unflagging energy, a comfortable house in Mayfair, an income provided by one means or another, and a position in Society not indeed at the peak, not by any means unassailable, but somewhere inside the fringe.

Doris had arrived at least as far as she could ever have hoped to do. It was a performance not to be despised. Her success showed what could be done, even in that age when social and moral barriers were stiffer than they are today, by one whose life, like her tongue, was unrestrained, who came from a good family, who had exceptional good looks and an ability to wear the clothes and jewels which affectionate suitors showered on her; who was, above all, a woman of high intelligence.

It is easy to see why Valentine, brought up on the beauty and disillusioned wisdom of Forzanne, was captivated by Doris, who was pretty, worldly-wise and (as Lord Beaverbrook testified) good-natured. Where a beautiful woman was concerned his good sense, such as it was, deserted him, and in a whirl of emotions he was ready to forget that there were other factors in life besides pleasure. For instance, pride.

Love is one thing, Marriage another. He should have known.

Valentine fell in with Doris when his love affair with the rich and beautiful Baroness de Forest was coming to an end. He was living at the time in the International Sportsman's Club in Grosvenor House. Doris had a house round the corner, for which, it was said, Sir Edward MacKay Edgar, a financier of the period, was paying the rent.

'Mike' Edgar, as he was called, was a colourful figure, a

Canadian with strong infusions of North American Indian blood. He was born in Montreal in 1876 and was as a young man translated to London after making a fortune stock-broking in Canada. As a merchant banker in the City, he was eventually involved in deals which overstrained his resources. After some spectacular benefactions he became a baronet in 1920; five years later, his affairs were 'involved' and eventually a dividend of 10½d in the £ was paid to his creditors. He died in 1934.

Castlerosse's marriage to Doris occurred three years after the first tremor in Edgar's fortunes. Castlerosse had very soon become a regular visitor to the flat in Deanery Street. One day John Gordon asked him, 'Why don't you go and live in Deanery Street, Valentine?' Valentine shook his head. It was out of the question. The reason? He explained patiently that the Deanery Street flat had a great defect: it had two steps down to the lavatory.

But in spite of the entreaties of his friends, the tears of his mother, the predictions and threats of Lord Revelstoke, Valentine married Doris. Why?

He had written very sensibly and with insight about marriage. 'Marrying for money often means spiritual bankruptcy. Marrying for social position is a cul-de-sac. Marrying to please others is, like a life insurance, also for the benefit of others. But marrying because you love a woman is right, reasonable and justifiable.' And he had concluded, 'Where there is marriage without love, there will be love without marriage.'

What were the proportions of love and other ingredients in the Castlerosse marriage? It is hard to say.

But the basic motive is hardly in dispute. Valentine married Doris because he was in love with her. Of that there is no doubt. There is reason to think that he remained in love with her all his life.

She was a woman of extraordinary sexual appeal – and a remarkable freedom of morals. In an age when men were allowed some licence and women were expected to conform, at least outwardly, Doris insisted in claiming the rights of the male. She was before her time. Finally, she united beauty with an intellect of disconcerting acuteness. The combination was bound to be irresistible to Valentine, who was himself a very clever man.

But how did she approach her new enterprise? It is certain that she was fond of Valentine, perhaps even in love with him. It was not the case that hers was one of those strong characters to whom the sentiments of love and loyalty are alien. On the contrary. They had been present – but life had been too hard and exacting a journey. And, from the beginning, married life with Valentine was difficult. For instance, there was Lord Beaverbrook, and there was her new husband's family . . .

When the news of the marriage in Hammersmith Registry Office broke on the Kenmare household, Lady Kenmare was in the forefront of the ensuing battle. She had expected little good from her eldest son but this was worse than anything that had gone before. In the hour of disaster, she clung to any straw of comfort. Hearing that the wedding had taken place in a registry office, she said, as a good Catholic, ' Thanks be to God, then it is no marriage.'

Soon afterwards Tim Healy, who reigned over Ireland from the vice-regal lodge in Dublin, heard the news from his friend Lord Beaverbrook. His reaction was different. ' Thanks be to God, the woman is a Catholic,' he said. This was not so, however. The de le Vingne clan in Belgium might be Catholics but Doris was a Protestant.

A minor problem now arose; how was the news to be broken to the public? What was to be the form of the announcement? Lady Kenmare, Lord Beaverbrook and Lord Castlerosse consulted together at a meeting arranged by Beaverbrook.

Lady Kenmare opened the discussion by declaring that she would never receive ' this woman ', a promise which, incidentally, she kept; nor would Doris ever be allowed to visit Killarney. She went on to say that Valentine was making the scandal worse by keeping it secret. It must be announced at once. They would draft a formula for which kind Lord Beaverbrook would secure suitable publicity. Valentine consented. But the matter did not end there.

On the contrary, it simply moved on from the plane of family drama to the plane of pure comedy – as incidents in Valentine's life were apt to do.

What was to be the form and wording of the announcement? Lady Kenmare said that it should say that the marriage had been 'celebrated'. This, one might have thought, was satisfactory enough. But it did not satisfy Valentine. Purple with anger, shouting like a turkey cock, he insisted that the marriage had not been 'celebrated'. It had been 'solemnized'.

Lady Kenmare fought back, rejecting the idea that the statutory proceedings in a London registry office could be, in any sense, a 'solemnity'. At this point a heated dispute broke out between mother and son over the exact meanings of English words. The New Oxford Dictionary was produced. Chambers' Dictionary came into play. So did Webster's. Quotations were swopped. In the course of this controversy, the original cause of the quarrel was forgotten. Incidentally, Valentine was in the right. The marriage certificate plainly declares that the marriage was 'solemnized'.

In spite of her anger, Lady Kenmare gave her son a motherly peck as she left, although she said to Lord Beaverbrook at the front door, 'Never will she enter my house while I am there.'

At this time, Valentine made one of his rare excursions into philosophy. Three months after Doris Delavigne married him, her brother Dudley became engaged to be married. Hearing the news in Biarritz, Valentine wrote his brother-in-law a letter which breathed affection, wit and wordly wisdom. It is one of the most sprightly products of his talent in this vein:

My dear Dudley,
>   Fine! excellent! A million congratulations.
>   But!
>   How are you going to live?
>   Do you propose making money?
>   Remember you probably won't –

Every young man in love always says he is going to make a fortune till eventually the bankruptcy proceedings coincide with the divorce petition.

In any case, you are not going to make a fortune overnight and what are you going to do in the meanwhile? Now Dudley! make your situation clear – don't write up the assets – only a fool does that. When I was a boy and owed £10,000 I always told my father I owed £20,000. When eventually my debts came to be paid my father felt that he had really made £10,000 and all was well.

Young men are like old men – a little vain – so I therefore propose to draw up your balance sheet for you:

Assets		*Debits*
cash in hand	nil	dances too well
	remember	
reversionary	death duties	
interests	cut things in	
	half	
earning power	doubtful	
goodwill	immense	

Remember what your fiancée calls nothing, you and I call a fortune. And don't be deceived by any promises of economy. Doris thinks she pays her own way, has become miserly, yet I can tell you that her casual expenses cost me £100 a week.

The Castlerosses at the Chateau de l'Horizon, a Riviera villa belonging to American actress Maxine Elliott

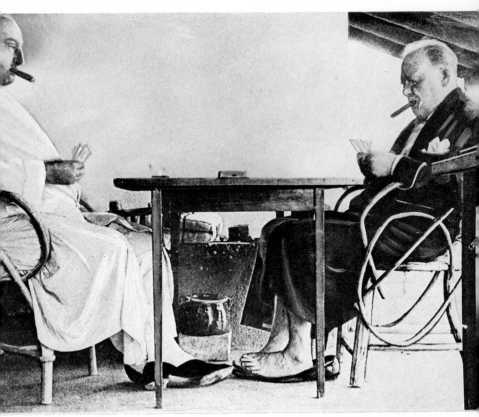

Lord Castlerosse plays cards with Winston Churchill at the Chateau de l'Horizon

Above The then Prince of Wales walking with Lord Castlerosse at St Andrews golf course in 1933

Opposite left Castlerosse at the Phoenix Park Races, Dublin

Opposite top Lord Castlerosse with Lord Beaverbrook and a young companion

Castlerosse takes his friend film producer Robert Kane deer-stalking on his estate in Killarney

Lord Castlerosse, by now Sixth Earl of Kenmare, marries his second wife, Enid Lady Furness, at Brompton Oratory in 1943

Rich people, especially if they have made money them-selves, always think that their children who they have soaked in luxury, can by the stroke of a wand or the sig-nature of a marriage register go back to the simple pleas-ures of their youth.

I can tell you it's impossible.

I see from your letter to Doris, who by way of economy managed to buy 12 dresses in Paris the day before yester-day, that you are desperately in love.

Like always happens, you will have to fight for your position.

You've got no money and you probably won't make any to speak of – very few people do.

Cut your cloth accordingly and remember that, where-as money has never made anybody happy, the lack of it has made the hell of a lot of people unhappy – and also another word of advice.

Marriages that start in heaven usually end in night clubs.

Would you like to go to Killarney on your honeymoon – it's a romantic spot.

Yours Valentine.

Thus eloquent in giving the sensible advice which he him-self was incapable of taking, Valentine composed a document worthy of Mr Micawber at his repentant best.

Beaverbrook was incensed by his friend's absurd and, as he thought, wrong-headed behaviour in marrying. For a time, then, Valentine was banned from Stornoway House, Lord Beaverbrook's home in London. But the estrangement between the two men did not last very long after the mar-riage. The bonds between them were too strong. And very soon Beaverbrook gleaned from watchful informants that for Valentine the nuptial seas were proving stormy.

There were disputes between the Castlerosses about trivial matters like money and more serious matters like men. On one occasion, when Valentine was financially embarrassed, Doris sold her house in Deanery Street to pay his debts.

Neither Valentine nor Doris found it easy to put aside the habits and diversions of the past. Neither had the slightest intention of doing so. Valentine had his clubs, his golf, his work as a journalist. Doris had her devotees, an enthusiastic if changeable band.

Sometimes Valentine stayed at his club; sometimes Doris shared the flat with a friend. It was impossible for her to change what had become her way of life, especially when Castlerosse, who had troubles enough with his own debts, could not pay hers. In these circumstances, it was inevitable that sooner or later Beaverbrook should be drawn into the affairs of the couple.

Doris met him with a brain almost as quick as his own. When he reproached her over her behaviour, she replied, ' Max, I would have you know that an Englishwoman's bed is her castle.' In a battle of wits, Lady Castlerosse could hold her own with the most formidable opponents.

The relationship between Valentine and Doris was more complex than love and quite different from friendship. It seemed that he hated her and yet was obsessed by her. He could convince himself that, already, she was beginning to lose her looks; he pretended to think that, on the marriage certificate, a false date had been given for her birth.

But Doris's smartness remained; her ability to command dresses, a dozen at a time, from the most fashionable couturiers of the day – and the open-handedness with which, when she had worn them once or twice, she would pass them on to young friends who did not have her resources. But, to the hypercritical eye of a man whose judgement was warped by jealousy, she was already beginning to fade.

As for Valentine, he too was suffering a physical change, although of a different order. He would have liked to be the great seducer, irresistible to women. When he found that

his success in this way fell short of his hopes, and that sometimes his closest friends stole his girls from him, he took
refuge in gluttony.

Gluttony, at the table and with the bottle, exacts a price
of its own. Valentine began to swell; he grew corpulent,
enormous; soon he was a figure of fun. The time was not far
off when he announced that he had given up going to the
cinema, because of the ' discomfort of the seats '. Later on, in
the cinema at Killarney, a spacious armchair was installed
for his use.

By the early Thirties all the fashionable world knew that
the Castlerosses were quarrelling. It was not a thing which
could be kept secret. Sometimes the noise of battle was
heard as Valentine and Doris hurled abuse at one another
over a table in some restaurant. When a friend accompanied
them to dinner, he was liable to find himself escorting Doris
back to her flat while Valentine went off to one of his clubs.
Sometimes the dispute passed from words to blows. Evening
shoes used as missiles flew across Doris's room in Deanery
Street.

Doris called in Lord Beaverbrook on one occasion to show
him the bruises which, she alleged, Valentine had caused.
Beaverbrook sent for Castlerosse and upbraided him furiously. After enduring this storm of indignation for a few
minutes, Valentine pulled up his trouser leg. There were the
marks of a great bite in his calf. ' That's what she did to
me,' he protested.

Beaverbrook was impressed by the sight. However, he said,
' Even this is no reason for you to hammer Doris like that.'
' But damn it, Max,' said Castlerosse, ' she would not let go!'

Beaverbrook's advice was terse. ' Live amicably with your
wife,' he wrote, ' or leave her.' But it seemed that Valentine
was incapable of accepting either half of this wise counsel.

On another occasion, when Castlerosse had reason to suppose that his wife was receiving a rich young baronet in his
absence, he waited in ambush in the dark street outside her

house. In due course the baronet arrived, waited until he saw Doris's signal and then approached the front door.

Valentine loomed up out of the shadows, enormous, dark with rage and brandishing an Irish blackthorn stick. With this he proceeded to give the baronet a merciless hiding. Hearing the noise, Doris ran downstairs into the street, adding her screams of ' Murder ' to the trumpetings of Valentine and the thuds of the stick.

That quiet Mayfair street had in its time heard many a fracas of this kind. But rarely in modern times have the indignant husband, the chastised lover and the erring wife made such a rumpus. Valentine enjoyed himself thoroughly. Probably all three of them did.

Against one young friend of his wife's he bore a lasting and savage grudge. Randolph Churchill not only became enamoured of Doris but, on one occasion, even had the bad taste to ring Castlerosse up from Doris's flat. As if this were not enough, he went so far as to dispute with Castlerosse the command of conversation at Valentine's dinner table. Such a challenge inevitably brought out the worst in Valentine. Once, when Churchill was attacking some statesman of an earlier generation, Castlerosse interrupted, ' Young man, it will be time enough to start abusing others when you have stopped abusing yourself.'

One evening at the Kit-Kat Club there was a violent scene between the two men. Randolph complained bitterly of the gossip-writers and declared that he was about to form a society to exclude them from parties. Valentine asked him what he thought of a book which Beaverbrook had published not long before* which was, as it chanced, a serious work on modern political history.

' It is the book of a sneak-guest,' said Randolph, who knew very well how close was the friendship between Beaverbrook and Castlerosse. Valentine lost his temper at that point and angry words were exchanged. He said that Winston

* *Politicians and the War* (Vol 1, Butterworth; Vol 2, Lane).

Churchill had murdered a quarter of a million men at the Dardanelles.

When Randolph made an angry retort, Castlerosse shouted, 'For two pins, I'd hit you.'

'Don't do that,' said Randolph, suddenly quiet and deadly. 'I'm not your wife.'

It was the climax to an ill-tempered evening but, as it chanced, it was not the end of the quarrel.

A few days later, Lord Castlerosse published an article in the *Daily Express* headed 'Sons of famous men'. 'All the young pigeons,' it began, 'are aping the habits and the fine feathers of peacocks. These pigeons are the sons of eminent fathers and they are basking in the shade of a parental halo . . .

'There is Randolph Churchill. He is a charming youth, but he is late in keeping appointments, and his powers are even more latent, though quite possibly they may also be there . . .'

Randolph, who probably detected the hand of Beaverbrook in the article, claimed the right of reply. It was granted. Not long before, Beaverbrook had rejected an article of Randolph's on the subject of religion which Beaverbrook, as a son of the manse, thought should not be published in one of his newspapers. Now Beaverbrook said, 'You can't attack God in the *Daily Express*, but you may attack Castlerosse.'

When Churchill's article appeared it was, as might have been expected, heavy-handed and in bad taste. Lord Castlerosse, it said:

came home after the war to a different England from the one he had left. It was no longer enough to be a slim-waisted exquisite, flitting around the salons. He was faced with the necessity of earning a living.

Lord Castlerosse is a scion of a family not only famous but dominant in the City. They gave him advantages denied to most young men; they placed him in a lucrative

City sinecure, but, alas, he gossiped himself out of a job . . . So [the Stock Exchange] thrust him upon Lord Beaverbrook . . .

Lord Castlerosse has principally endeared himself to his friends because he is supposed to be amusing. I have always found him more amusing to look at than to listen to, but what a tragedy it is, as he is supposed to be a wit, to have a wife who is so much more amusing than himself . . . Why did he write this article? The answer is very simple. He is jealous.

At the age of forty-one, said Churchill, ten years of sycophancy had brought Castlerosse only to the height – the low height – of a gossip-writer.

After this exchange of broadsides between the two rivals, the battle died down. Perhaps Lord Beaverbrook had decided that the public had enjoyed enough of this exhibition of aristocratic bad behaviour.

By this time it was obvious that the Castlerosses' marriage was heading for the rocks. Beaverbrook himself was anxious to relieve either party of the company of a distasteful consort. Yet the matter was not so easy to arrange as all that.

There was a moment when Doris, weary of Valentine, agreed that she would divorce her husband if only Beaverbrook would take him to Canada. But there were times when she thought that divorce was a rose not without its thorns.

In 1933, when Sir John Lavery was painting her portrait, she was worried about the picture's prospects of getting into the Royal Academy, a process which she seemed to think was rather like being presented at Buckingham Palace. 'If I were divorced,' she asked Lavery, 'it would not make any difference, would it, Sir John?'

Lady Lavery, who was very fond of Valentine, had a more dispassionate view of Doris, who she said had some of the same qualities as Ramsay MacDonald, above all the gift of durability, permanence, ability to survive rebuffs and unpopularity. Valentine's opinion of the portrait was incisive. ' It may be art,' he said, ' but it isn't Doris.' It was, in fact, a brilliant portrait.

The time came when Valentine employed detectives to report on his wife's conduct. They were not always lucky. At one time, the spies reported that Doris had at last been trapped in the Ritz Hotel, Paris, with a man.

Disappointment followed. The news was imparted to Valentine. He telephoned back: ' Yes. She has a man with her. But, you bloody fool, it's me.'

On another occasion, Valentine was staying in the Hyde Park Hotel under strict orders that on no account was he to see his wife, who had been detected in the company of a man. Doris, who as often happened had found out what was afoot, was by no means dismayed. She went to the Hyde Park Hotel, made for Valentine's room, took off all her clothes, got into bed and rang for the valet.

When the valet arrived, he had before him the evidence that Lord Castlerosse had condoned his wife's conduct.

If jealousy is a proof of love, then undoubtedly Valentine was in love with Doris and remained her slave.

At last the day came in 1938 when Castlerosse, apparently quite unabashed, shared the news of the failure of his marriage with his public. ' I do not know whether you noticed it,' he wrote in the ' Log ', ' but last week my divorce was made absolute.'

When someone remarked that it was strange that divorce should cost so much more than marriage, he replied, ' Not at all. It's worth more.' Doris's verdict on the marriage was, ' We were married for ten years. We lived together for one.'

Valentine was one of those men of whom it is said, ' He should not have married.' It seemed certain that whatever wife he chose would be doomed to misery in the shadow of so boisterous and egocentric a husband. What could not have been predicted was that his fancy would hit upon a woman able to inflict at least as much pain as she received.

It is easy enough to say that Valentine should not have married Doris Delavigne. But whom, then, should he have married? The task of finding a wife for Valentine was one from which any person of commonsense would certainly have shrunk.

She would – this theoretical lady whom Valentine did not find – require to have all the negative virtues and, in addition, a well-protected private income, safeguarded by trustees capable of keeping the money out of Lord Castlerosse's hands. She would need to be a good sort, a good hostess, an amiable conversationalist, shutting her ears to the more outrageous of her husband's stories and her eyes to the more flagrant of his infidelities.

When Valentine disappeared suddenly on one of his frequent expeditions in Lord Beaverbrook's retinue, she would be expected to stay at home. So, like a wise woman, she would be well-advised to have a circle of friends of her own.

It would be a good idea if she were, or speedily became, a Catholic. That would have pleased Lady Kenmare. It would be even better if she were to produce some children. That would have pleased Lord Kenmare, and in time Valentine, not normally partial to the patter of little feet, would have learnt to play the role of father with dignity.

He was a negligent but wildly generous godfather, remembered for his extravagant tips. To one of his godsons, the Hon. Alexander Thynne (now Viscount Weymouth), he sent a pedigree dog of his own raising as a birthday present, accompanying it by one of his rare and charming letters:

My dear Alexander,

I hope you got the dog Bran quite safely. To start with, I am afraid you will find him very shy but if you feed him on cream, champagne, frogs and young clergymen –

the clergymen to be boiled very lightly in oil – you will find that his health and temperament will show great improvement!

During Lent he prefers the left leg of a Bishop grilled and devilled.

From your devoted godfather,

Valentine.

Perhaps, once he had got used to the idea of paternity, he would have settled down and become a whimsical, difficult but delightful father. But the matter was never put to the test.

The task of finding a suitable wife for Valentine was one which men would have found beyond their powers and which women would have revelled in.

The ideal Lady Castlerosse would have been a woman of whom people said with a sigh, 'Poor—!'

The real Lady Castlerosse had few of the requisite qualifications. And nobody ever said 'Poor Doris!'

Valentine fell seriously ill a few months before his divorce. His chief anxiety at that time was lest there should be any misunderstanding about the cause of his illness. 'I want to make it quite clear, if I die, that it was due to the green streptococcus and not to anything else. I don't want to have Doris going about boasting that she broke my heart.'

But this very insistence seemed to show that he had been hurt. It might be irrational in one who had, after all, known from the beginning what sort of woman Doris was. It might be perverse in one to whom marriage seemed to have made no difference in his attitude to life and morals. It was plainly against all the rules of the cynical society in which he had been brought up. Nevertheless, the fact would hardly be disputed.

In some ultimate cranny of his being, he remained in love with Doris and was therefore liable to suffer. He was boisterous, outrageous, an elephant at large in the jungle of Mayfair. But he was an elephant with a thin skin.

13

Lord Castlerosse was a man with his own ideas about how life should be conducted; for instance, about where he should live and how he should dress.

Thus, his suite at the International Sportsman's Club was furnished according to his ideas of what a gentleman's flat should look like. As might be expected, his ideas were original and logical. When his admiring nephew, later Lord de Vesci, then a subaltern in the Guards, paid him a visit, he was surprised to find that in the centre of the room a huge block of ice was standing. It was encased in wire-netting from which hung bottles of every possible make of brandy and liqueur. One wall of the room was occupied by books; another by boxes of cigars, scores of them, stacked one on top of another. Thus, three of the occupant's main interests were conspicuously represented in the décor.

From this eyrie Valentine would sally forth to see the boxing match of the night, to play cards at White's, to take some beautiful woman to dinner and, as the night wore on, to take himself to Stornoway House and place his brandy bottle on Lord Beaverbrook's dining table.

As for his views about clothes, these were well established in the course of some court proceedings of the time.

'Lord Castlerosse is not an unreasonable man,' conceded the tailor in the witness box, 'but he has funny sartorial ideas.'

It occurred during the hearing of a lawsuit in March 1933 when Castlerosse was sued by Messrs Oakes, of Savile Row, for £75 for two dress suits. Castlerosse, in resisting the claim, pleaded that the suits were misfits. Oakes said that, if indeed (which they denied) the suits did not fit, it was because his lordship kept fidgeting during the fittings. To this charge Valentine had an effective answer, ' As to not standing still,' he said, drawing himself to his full, imposing height, ' I have been in the Guards.' And he spoke contemptuously of the suits as fit only for the zoo.

Oakes, in order to demonstrate how difficult a customer he was, spoke of the unorthodox materials he had chosen for his dinner suits: one of blue herring-bone and one of blue tropical hopsack. In the end, neither side could claim a victory. But judgement was given in Oakes's favour for £22 10s for the waistcoats. Not all tailors were as lucky as they.

In his taste in clothes, Valentine rebelled against the commonplace. In his opinion, clothes were not a uniform imposed on humanity by some unseen quartermaster. They were one of the ways in which a man expressed his personality and made his contribution to the variety and interest of this beautiful world.

Where his father had been correct and elegant, Valentine was flamboyant. His tweeds were salmon pink or rainbow-hued, a surprising spectacle in the Irish countryside. And to see him in London in his fur coat, sable-collared and mink-lined, was to have a vision of opulence itself.

It seemed that few men could be rich enough to afford such magnificence. Certainly Valentine was not one of them. This did not deter him from ordering suits by the dozen and shirts by the gross. When the moment came to pay, there would always, somehow, be money to meet the bill. For God was in His heaven above and nearer and more immediate, Lord Beaverbrook was in Stornoway House, Cleveland Row, St James's.

In the Royal Academy exhibition of 1935, a Sickert portrait of Castlerosse attracted some attention, notably among those who did not know that the model had not sat for the artist. Sickert had been content to work from a couple of snapshots of his sitter. However, the portrait was undoubtedly striking. But the *Tailor and Cutter*, in criticizing it, paid more attention to the clothes than to the man.

'There is a collar on the waistcoat,' it said disapprovingly, 'and some tricksy, elfish gilt buttons and from the pocket hangs a dainty ribbon. The noble lord's eyes are closed, but there is a seraphic smile on his face.' This expression was all the easier for Valentine to assume since he was not paying for the portrait, which was a commission to the artist from Sir James Dunn, the Canadian financier.

With such ever-present assurance, divine and human, Beaverbrook and Dunn, Valentine could continue on his way living the philosophy which he expressed with such feeling: 'My dear fellow, not to do a thing you want to do because you cannot afford it is quite absurd.' In his own perverse way, then, he had something of the masterful way of the Barings with money.

He gambled and lost. He gambled and won and then squandered his winnings. In either case there was always someone reluctant, but in the end willing to pay – his father, a man with Victorian notions about meeting one's obligations; his mother, who in spite of her severe words could rarely resist his wheedling; or Beaverbrook, who knew that Castlerosse had become one of the most substantial properties in his newspaper empire. In the last analysis, none of these three was prepared to see Valentine made bankrupt. All of them suffered.

At the end of 1937, Beaverbrook wrote from Miami Beach to E. J. Robertson, managing director of the Express Newspapers. It was in the midst of one of the worst of Valentine's financial crises:

Castlerosse . . . I am determined to help him to the extent of several thousand pounds in the hope that he will get some assistance from his mother, or make another marriage of a fortunate nature, with the money in the pool.

But we must give that help grudgingly and with such restrictions as to make his demands as small as his circumstances will permit.

You might let me know what view you take of the impending disappearance of his column from the *Sunday Express*. For, of course, bankruptcy will terminate his labours. He is the type that must make a world of illusion for himself. And if his world of make-believe should collapse he will be incapable of doing work for the *D[aily], E[xpress]*.

The truth was that, about that time, the object of all this friendly solicitude was looking beyond the sphere of journalism. The wind from an ampler sea was filling his sails. In the meantime he felt free to commit new follies.

One day he was going down the steps of the St James's Club in Piccadilly after a disastrous session at the tables, where the play was notoriously high. He ran into Lord Queensberry to whom he confided the sad story of his misfortunes.

'Don't tell Max,' he added.

'Why not?' asked Queensberry.

'Because it's bad for his health,' said Castlerosse blandly and continued on his way to the pavement below where his car was waiting at the kerb and his chauffeur, Godfrey, was holding the door open.

'It isn't gold that alters a man's character,' says one of the characters in *The Treasure of the Sierra Madre*. 'It's the power gold gives him; and that's why people get excited when they see gold.'

Nobody was ever more excited than Castlerosse about money. His was the excitement of the big gambler, a loser who could not resist coming back for more punishment and, when he won, a wonderful spender. I do not think that gold – its presence or its absence – ever altered his character, although it certainly made a difference to his equanimity. But in financial defeat he was downcast only for a moment. The cork does not sink in the storm.

As for 'the power gold gives him,' money only brought one gift that Castlerosse valued – the power to spend, that is, to squander. 'The cruel thing about wealth,' he said, ' is that a man must part with it to enjoy it.' Nobody has ever had more enjoyment out of parting with it. There was something childish and absurd about his handling of money which aroused the anguished pity of the rich men whose company he loved. Lord Beaverbrook, at a time when Valentine's extravagance had helped to bring the Kenmare estates into difficulties, said that, above all, Castlerosse should not be given control of them.

Not everybody shared Beaverbrook's scepticism about Valentine's acumen. Once Beaverbrook asked his son Max, 'What would you do if I died? To whom would you turn?' The boy answered without hesitation, 'Valentine.' Beaverbrook, astonished by the reply, told Castlerosse about it.

'Why were you astonished?' asked Valentine.

'Well,' said Beaverbrook, 'you take no physical exercise. You are not an out-of-door type like Mike Wardell!*

The reason was irrelevant, as Valentine could have pointed out. But Max's reply was probably prompted not so much by admiration for Valentine's business qualities as by liking for his father's friend and respect for his broad human sympathy. In fact, Beaverbrook himself often consulted Castlerosse in matters of policy.

One evening, Beaverbrook told the novelist, William Gerhardi (perhaps mischievously), ' If you want to be great friends with Valentine, just ask him how much he earns.'

* Captain, now Brigadier, Michael Wardell, at that time managing director of the *Evening Standard*.

Gerhardi did as he was told and Valentine was furious. To him, there was something distasteful, almost shameful, about money that was the fruit of honest toil. On the other hand, if money were won at the tables or by some successful speculation it was a tribute to his cunning. He could boast of it, exaggerate it and squander it.

After Beaverbrook had helped him out of a bad scrape, Valentine wrote, ' I promise absolutely never to go again to a moneylender under any circumstances.' But, if moneylenders were banished, other kinds of creditors were not. At the end of 1938 Castlerosse's debts amounted to £1,319 16s 2d, the main items being: cigars, £330; boots, £72; shirts, £250; tailor, £171; golf clubs, £24; wine, £166; Orleans Club coffee room, £117.

On one occasion, there was an outburst of jubilation in the Beaverbrook camp. From mouth to mouth the joyful tidings ran, ' Valentine has opened a savings bank account!' But, alas, it proved to be a false dawn.

After the Great Slump which burst on Wall Street in 1929, a profound depression had settled on the world's bourses. It was a time in which only the very cunning or the unscrupulous could make money and only the very rich were confident of surviving. As Valentine wrote to his friend, Beaverbrook, ' The only story of prosperity in this bankrupt world is that of the two fleas who won the pools and bought a dog.'

Once or twice, however, in the Stock Exchange or in the Casino, he was fortunate, too. One day Lord Beaverbrook telephoned to John Gordon, ' I hear that Valentine has bought a dog track.' ' Yes, he has,' said Gordon. ' That is quite true.' Over the telephone came the sounds of Beaverbrook's dismay. Once more, it seemed, his prodigal friend was about to plunge into ruinous complications.

' Get him out of that dog track,' said Beaverbrook to Gordon. Gordon spoke reassuringly. ' It is quite all right. There is nothing to worry about. Valentine bought the track yesterday morning and sold it last night at a profit of £26,000.'

The coup had the simplest explanation in the world. In the morning the dog track had not been licensed and Castlerosse had obtained from his golfing crony, General Critchley, who was the chairman of the Greyhound Racing Association, a pledge that by nightfall it would be licensed. And so it was. When evening came the licensed dog track was worth much more than it had been in the morning and Castlerosse made his profit. How long the money would be likely to remain in his bank account is another matter. What can safely be assumed is that little of it found its way to his creditors!

On another occasion, Valentine was saved from a serious involvement by good fortune and well-informed friends.

Sometime in 1928, or perhaps early in the following year, he fell in with Clarence Hatry. This man was a brilliant financier with a fatal weakness still unsuspected by his admirers. He had a wonderful gift for 'selling' an idea to the public and, which is usually harder, to the financiers. Thus he brought off several large-scale mergers which have proved to be of lasting usefulness. Allied Ironfounders is one example.

Naturally, Hatry expected to make an enormous profit from his part in the financial dealings associated with the mergers. The trouble was that he was greedy and vain.

His most ambitious venture was aimed at bringing about an amalgamation of steel companies. He thought he could finance this vast operation alone by borrowing from the banks and from other sources. At the end of the story he would be able to recoup himself by a public issue, and he expected to make a great deal of money. But as it turned out this could not be.

The value of the shares which Hatry had put up as collateral to the banks fell heavily, thanks to the slump on Wall Street of which Castlerosse, a few months earlier, had heard the first sinister whispers during his visit to New York. Hatry now turned to other methods in order to meet his commitments.

About this time he fell in with Castlerosse, a man of title, a public figure of some consequence, and one whose affluent appearance and breezy manner – to say nothing of his relations in Baring Brothers – could be of immense value to Hatry at this crisis in his fortunes.

It is possible that Hatry fell under the spell of Valentine's enormous charm. It is certain that Valentine was fascinated by the financier's brilliance. After a few expensive lunches in the Great Eastern Hotel, Hatry offered Castlerosse a directorship at a salary of £10,000.

A few months before, Castlerosse in his 'Log' had noted with disapproval that peers were forsaking their place in the House of Lords 'for the chairmanship of strange affairs which will no doubt eventually be explained in the Courts'. Nevertheless, Castlerosse was tempted by Hatry's proposition, especially as he had just added Doris's expensive tastes to his own.

Mr S. W. Alexander, financial editor of the *Sunday Express*, tried to dissuade him from accepting. Others did the same. Although there was nothing against Clarence Hatry, yet there hung about all his enterprises a faint odour of the meretricious. There was altogether too much glitter about them. But all the warnings to Castlerosse were in vain. The ten thousand pounds' directorship completely dazzled him. He would not listen to the voices of caution.

Then something happened which changed the picture dramatically. Sitting in his office in the City one day in the late summer of 1929, Alexander had a telephone call from a man who spoke in a nervous voice and claimed to be an employee of Hatry's. He had an important story to tell. Alexander invited him to come along to his office and tell it. The man was much too scared to do so. He said, 'I dare not be seen coming into your office.'

' Do you know me by sight ?' asked Alexander. The man on the telephone did.

' Very well,' said Alexander, ' meet me at the taxi rank in Liverpool Street Station at such and such a time exactly. I shall be getting into a taxi. You jump in beside me.'

And so it was. The two went off together.

The taxi drove several times round Hyde Park while the Hatry employee, who had been in the employment of the financier for several years, poured out an extraordinary story.

Hatry and his confederates were forging Warwickshire County Loan certificates in a secret engraving plant they had set up, somewhere in Kent. These certificates, which were for large amounts but not in great numbers, were then lodged as collateral for the loans Hatry had obtained! It was as simple as that.

During the taxi journey, Alexander was acquainted with the secret of one of the most impudent frauds in the records of the City of London. He advised his informant to consult a solicitor without delay. Then he returned to his office.

One of his first thoughts was to tell Castlerosse what was the real position of Hatry's finances.

Castlerosse was incredulous. Hatry, he protested, was a man of complete honesty and exceptional acumen. It was quite unthinkable that he would be party to so blatant a fraud. But he held back from committing himself for long enough. While he did so, the scandal was made public.

One day Hatry walked into a police station in the City. The crash which followed cost the City and the investing public about fourteen million pounds. But Castlerosse, thanks to Alexander's warning, was not one of Hatry's directors. He was, therefore, not one of the Hatry victims.

The Marquess of Winchester was not so lucky. He was already one of Hatry's directors. He was ruined.

In the tragi-comedy of Valentine's life, money is a main theme. Another is women.

He talked about them so much; wrote about them so often; made such a parade of his associations that some good judges have come to the conclusion that he would have liked to be a rake but was not one.

The truth seems to be otherwise. In spite of his increasingly grotesque appearance, Valentine never had much trouble in finding all the women he wanted. At one of Beaverbrook's parties, the prettiest women in the room were generally to be found at his feet. His appeal was − what exactly? Wit, high spirits; bursts of outrageous vulgarity; the goggling eye of the excited male. When to these gifts was added a more than Irish sentimentality then Valentine's appeal could be recognized as the formidable affair that it was. Eloquently and unblushingly he attacked a woman in her heart, which is her weakest and most susceptible part. And so he amused many women, charmed a few and enjoyed in his life the company of a series of beautiful mistresses.

14

How on earth, it may be asked, did a man like Beaverbrook who was not the most patient of mortals and was certainly not one to tolerate fools gladly, endure as much as he did at the hands of Castlerosse? Because of the deep affection between the two men. But on what was that affection based?

They were profoundly different in outlook and temperament. No two men could have been more so since the last Cavalier followed the last Roundhead into the shades. For instance, Beaverbrook respected money and Castlerosse pursued and despised it. Beaverbrook was fighting against a streak of anxiety in himself; he envied Valentine's insouciance.

And although it was irritating, galling, infuriating to be called upon so often to console the creditors of the prodigal, yet Beaverbrook could not help enjoying – as he could afford to do – the wry comedy of the situation. That he, the boy from the manse in New Brunswick who had wrested and wrestled his way to great wealth by ceaseless attention to the rules of financial prudence – that he should be paying the debts of this spendthrift, this jackass, this mountebank from the aristocracy – it was undeniably funny! There was in Beaverbrook a strong strain of masochistic pleasure.

Beaverbrook was aware, too, that Valentine, who irritated him so often to his face, was his pugnacious defender behind his back. As Bruce Lockhart remarked waspishly, Valentine's defence often took a form as injudicious and as embarrassing to his friend as could be imagined. But then, Bruce Lockhart was envious of the position Castlerosse held in Beaverbrook's affections.

So Castlerosse squandered and repented, promised reform, wept over his backslidings and came back to borrow again. He was like Maria Theresa of Austria, who wrung her hands with sorrow over the partition of Poland. Her fellow-robber, Frederick the Great, remarked, ' She wept – and she grabbed.' So it was with Castlerosse. As for Beaverbrook, he raged and paid.

From Castlerosse he received, after all, something which he valued even more than the weekly articles which were helping the *Sunday Express* up the circulation ladder. He was surrounded at Stornoway House and at Cherkley, his country house at Leatherhead, by a circle of friends – beautiful women, clever men, rising politicians and rowdy journalists. He was the sun of that rumbustious little solar system, the monarch of that Byzantine court. But a court demands more than a king, and Valentine brought it something which it needed.

He was its jester, witty and outrageous, bringing to the dining-room the latest scandal of the clubs, the newest story of disaster in the City, sparing no woman's blushes. Over and over again a sedate habitué like Bruce Lockhart was horrified by the freedom of Valentine's talk. But the girls, who might have been shocked, remained calm enough. Their cheeks were innocent of blushes. Beaverbrook did not seem to have heard. And Bruce Lockhart, morally outraged as he might be, came back at the first invitation to be shocked once more.

Round Beaverbrook there was a circle of mutually jealous courtiers. Thus Bruce Lockhart was jealous of Castlerosse and Castlerosse was jealous both of Brendan Bracken and Captain Michael Wardell. At the time when Castlerosse was in disfavour because of his marriage to Doris, Wardell enjoyed almost a monopoly of Beaverbrook's company. This did not go unnoticed by Castlerosse, who took his own way of avenging himself on his supplanter.

One day he met Frederick Lonsdale, the playwright, in Claridges. Lonsdale, who knew that Castlerosse was in disgrace, asked how Beaverbrook was.

'Haven't you heard?' said Castlerosse. 'Max's in jail.'

'Good God,' exclaimed Lonsdale. 'What did he do?'

'It happened at Cherkley,' Castlerosse explained. 'Max and Mike Wardell were dining together. It was even duller that night than usual. Max turned to the butler and said, "Bring me a magnum of champagne." When it came, Max looked at the label and then broke the bottle over Wardell's head. Wardell fell to the ground, dead.

'"Now," said Max to the butler. "Remove this body and bring me Lord Castlerosse."'

In a matter of hours the story was being repeated to Lord Beaverbrook, who did not fail to note the sly touch of 'Max looked at the label'. In a matter of days, Castlerosse was allowed once more to sparkle at the Cherkley dinner table.

The Beaverbrook circle, or 'the Cherkley set' as it was sometimes called, was a subject for envy to some who did not belong to it, and of disapproval to others. It was intensely exclusive and, like most groups of that kind, had its own interests, its own code of manners and almost its own language. The stranger who was invited to one of the Cherkley evenings or weekends often found himself still outside and not inside the magic circle. At Cherkley one man's whim was law.

Who belonged to the set? The membership varied from time to time as one or another temporarily came under the cloud of Beaverbrook's disapproval. But on the whole the solar system consisted of a group of inner planets, the more intimate and steadfast friends of the master – above all, Mrs Norton, a woman of exceptional wit and beauty, Lord

Castlerosse and Captain Wardell, an officer of the Tenth Hussars and a member of 'the Prince of Wales's set' until Lord Beaverbrook turned him into a newspaper executive. These enjoyed the privilege of a 'grace and favour' bedroom in Cherkley. Valentine bought a bed of exceptional size and strength and installed it in the room reserved for him.

There was Robert Bruce Lockhart, a diplomat in Moscow during the Russian Revolution, later (like Castlerosse) an unsuccessful banker, later still (and again like Castlerosse) a successful Beaverbrook journalist. Frequent but irregular attenders were Frederick Lonsdale, the dramatist, Frank Owen, politician and journalist and, most brilliant talker of all, Aneurin Bevan.

Then there was a confident and talkative young MP for Paddington named Brendan Bracken, a protégé of Winston Churchill's. Bracken was, among other things, one of the proprietors of the *Financial Times*. He brought to Beaverbrook's table the latest gossip from the House of Commons as well as the talk in various noble homes which he had just left. Nothing was more likely to endear him to Lord Beaverbrook – or to rouse a sense of rivalry in Castlerosse.

At one time, the *Financial Times* began to attack Lord Beaverbrook, a man who believed that counter-attack was the best form of self-defence. He considered ways in which he might hit back at Bracken who, he suspected, was the instigator of the attack. Then he called in Castlerosse and Mr Percy Hoskins, crime reporter of the *Daily Express*.

In those days, many people believed that Bracken was an illegitimate son of Winston Churchill. It was a legend which Bracken appeared to encourage. What was the truth? At the dinner table at Stornoway House, Beaverbrook said to Hoskins: 'I want you to look into this fellow's history and find out what the truth is.' Castlerosse helped himself to another glass of brandy and said, 'You want to go over to Ireland. That is where you will find the truth. When you go over there, come and visit me at my house in Killarney.'

Hoskins went over to Dublin and there he met Oliver St John Gogarty. Gogarty advised him: 'You go to a place called Templemore. You will find it all there. After that you can go on to Castlerosse's place in Killarney.'

Templemore is in Tipperary, about half-way between Dublin and Killarney. Hoskins set off there without any loss of time, and found that it was a tiny village of about a hundred people. Looking up the reference books he saw that on the outskirts of the town was the Devil's Bit Mountain. He put on a hiker's costume and ran up and down for a while until his heart was racing.

Then he went into an old doctor's house and said, 'I am very worried. I have been trying to climb this mountain and my heart is racing.' The doctor examined him and said, 'At your time of life you shouldn't be climbing mountains.' Hoskins then said, 'It's funny I should be taken ill here because this is where my Member of Parliament for Paddington was born.'

'You mean Brendan?' the doctor said.

'Yes, Mr Bracken.'

'I brought him into the world. His father was the local stone mason and his brother is up the road now, carving a tombstone for one of my patients.'

And for the next half an hour the doctor poured out the family history of the Brackens.

That was as near as Mr Hoskins got to Lord Castlerosse's home in Killarney! He went back to Dublin where he lunched every day with Gogarty and W. B. Yeats. For the next week he sent Lord Beaverbrook a daily instalment of the progress of his quest. So during an agreeable stay in Dublin he span out the story he had gleaned from half an hour's talk with the Templemore doctor.

Beaverbrook was at times the victim of Valentine's stories. Once, said Castlerosse, he was dining with Max and D., a beautiful lady of unimpeachable reputation. The company was less jovial that evening than usual. The reasons were simple. Max had a pimple on his leg and feared that he had syphilis. D. had a pimple on her breast and thought she had cancer.

Max, having an inclination towards hypochondria, telephoned his doctor, Lord Horder, the most famous physician of the day. 'When Horder came, this is what he saw,' said Castlerosse, telling the story, 'D. was stroking Max's leg. Max was stroking D.'s breast. And the only person really ill was myself, who had clap.'

The anecdote, which Valentine took enormous pleasure in circulating, may be taken as an example of his gift of outrageous invention. His power of repartee was quite equally coarse. One day Lady Astor, teasing him about his girth, patted his enormous stomach.

'If this was on a woman what would we think?'

'Half an hour ago,' said Valentine, 'it was.'

Invited by Beaverbrook one night to meet Lloyd George, Castlerosse refused point-blank. He was, he said, a South of Ireland Loyalist and Lloyd George was the man who had betrayed him and his friends to their enemies, the Irish Separatists. Nothing would induce him to meet such a man. Cooling down rapidly as the evening wore on, he abandoned this pose of a champion of rigid principles. He consented to meet Lloyd George.

Beaverbrook introduced him and said, 'Valentine, you must give L.G. a write-up in your "Log" next Sunday.'

Castlerosse turned his back and took two steps to the left, pirouetting like a ballet dancer. For a moment the nervous onlookers thought that he was about to insult the great man.

Instead he made a deep bow and said, 'For me to write up the man who won the war would be – if I may use a Catholic simile – like the village *curé* venturing to write up the Pope.' This revolting display of sycophancy made L.G. purr, but from that moment on he was in brilliant conversational form – when Valentine gave him a chance to speak.

After the elder statesman and his secretary had left, matters were rather different. Valentine's anecdotes about the man who had won the war became more and more ribald. But needless to say L.G. was given most favourable mention in 'The Londoner's Log' on the following Sunday, for Valentine, in spite of everything, always came to heel and wrote what was likely to find favour with his proprietor.

There was a strong vein of realism in him. For example, there was a Chaplin film in 1931 which Beaverbrook disliked. He had an antipathy to Chaplin, whether on the understandable, human ground that the actor was enjoying a success, and should therefore be pulled down, or because he thought it 'good journalism' to follow a line in opposition to that of the majority. Valentine saw the film, liked it but, without much ado, wrote a very amusing article criticizing it. No doubt Beaverbrook contributed some thought to the article. And, no doubt, Castlerosse enjoyed the collaboration.

Making an occasional concession of this sort to his employer, he was all the more free to express his own views and his own personality in his column. He was superficial and frivolous, as his public expected, but occasionally he was serious. Once he escorted blinded ex-soldiers to Ypres, and wrote a description of the journey. Beaverbrook sent him a telegram, 'If I did not know you so well, I should have been deeply moved.' It was, in fact, a very moving account and it was, as Beaverbrook knew very well, completely sincere.

Valentine was not always as respectful to the great as he had been to Lloyd George. He met H. G. Wells one evening at Beaverbrook's dinner table. Wells was holding forth about the inevitable collapse of capitalism and the coming revolution, while the other guests were almost falling under the table with boredom.

Valentine, who had drunk deeply, did not give up the fight. In his most genial tones he told Wells that he had been reading a book of Trotsky's in which a remark of Lenin's was quoted – 'Wells is a mutton-headed bourgeois.' At this, the dinner party livened considerably. Wells, nettled and embarrassed, said in his squeaky voice that Lenin had probably said, 'Wells has a lot of middle-class qualities.' The explanation was unconvincing. But from that moment onwards the dinner party heard less about the impending downfall of capitalism.

Castlerosse was, on the whole, surprisingly well-disciplined as a journalist. While he basked in praise and sulked over criticism, as writers do, generally speaking he could be relied on as a workman who was keeping one eye on the clock. However, his editors had some causes for dissatisfaction with him.

When John Gordon sent him to St Andrews to report the final of the Open Championship, he was there for not more than three days. But he found time not only to give an admirable account of the golf but also to buy 147 new golf clubs and four new golf bags. The bills for these were sent to the *Sunday Express*. Gordon, in compensation, took a set of the clubs for himself.

On one occasion when Castlerosse accompanied Beaverbrook to New York, he invited Gordon to White's Club for a drink before leaving. Gordon went, one reason being that he wished to be certain Castlerosse really would arrive at the boat train in time. As they sat in White's, drinking more and more champagne, Gordon became increasingly anxious. Finally he asked the porter at the club to call a taxi into which, with enormous difficulty, and at the very last minute, he bundled Castlerosse.

They arrived at the Waterloo departure platform after the guard had blown his whistle, and Gordon pushed Castlerosse into the rear carriage. Then he ran along the train where Beaverbrook was leaning out of a window looking anxiously along the platform. 'It's all right,' said Gordon breathlessly. 'I've got him into the last carriage in the train.'

Lord Beaverbrook's concern may, on this occasion, reasonably have been tinged with annoyance. He was angry with Valentine, who had been misbehaving, running into debt, making scenes in restaurants and so on. Beaverbrook said he would on no account take Valentine with him on the journey. His reputation was too bad. Valentine had pleaded, had promised to reform and had finally burst into tears. Then at last, Beaverbrook capitulated. 'I could never resist his tears,' he explained, although no doubt he had all along intended to take with him the man whom he regarded as the best, although not always the most reliable, travelling companion in the world.

On another crossing to New York, this time accompanied by both Gordon and Castlerosse, every night at dinner Beaverbrook used to guide the conversation towards some remote subject on which he would then hold forth, showing a deep knowledge of the most recondite matters. After three nights of this, Gordon and Castlerosse became suspicious. They sought out Beaverbrook's valet, an apparently frail but in reality tough little Cockney called Albert. 'What,' they asked him, 'has his lordship been reading lately?'

Albert showed them the books. Sure enough, they were on the subjects about which Beaverbrook had recently been so surprisingly knowledgeable. Then they said, 'What is he reading today, Albert? Let us borrow it.' Albert abstracted the book of the moment from Beaverbrook for a couple of hours, during which time Gordon and Castlerosse absorbed all its contents.

At dinner, that night, they held forth eloquently and at length on the subject. Their knowledge was encyclopaedic. When one of them faltered for a moment, the other took up the tale. Never was there such a deluge of information.

Impressed at first and then astounded by the display, Beaverbrook asked at last, 'Where did you learn all that?'

'From the book you were reading this afternoon,' said

Castlerosse, with that particular sweetness of enunciation which he reserved for such moments of triumph.

He was himself a man who read widely, if not deeply. On one Atlantic crossing in Beaverbrook's company, he took four hundred volumes in his baggage including the complete works of Rider Haggard, who at that time had become one of his favourite authors.

He liked to repeat Anatole France's saying, ' A man's brain is not adapted to the deep realities of life.' On his lips it had a sound of gravity and originality. Similarly he had the flattering gift of picking up a remark made by somebody in talk and making it the setting for ideas of his own. He was a great conversationalist rather than a great talker, with the gift of picking phrases and ideas from his reading and using them in a conversation with an impressive effect of wit and knowledge.

Unlike his fellow-Irishman, Oscar Wilde, he was not a great solo performer at the dinner table. For one thing, he was interested in eating and drinking as well as in talking. He excelled in the impertinent interruption of someone else's flow of words – the audacious aside; the improper jest. Particularly he took pleasure in deflating the pompous and disconcerting the *prime donne* of talk. Nobody better than he could add to the animation and excitement of a dinner table. For this Beaverbrook, if occasionally his victim, forgave him a great deal.

15

In Valentine, then, Lord Beaverbrook had discovered one of the best of companions. But like all things which are of the first quality, the price tag attached to the article was high. Lord Castlerosse knew his own value and had no compunction at all in exacting the appropriate payment.

On one occasion, when he was staying at the Carlton Hotel, Cannes, Lord Beaverbrook was dismayed to discover that his party had run up a bill for several hundreds of bottles of mineral water. He investigated and found that the bill was correct. The explanation was simple.

In a temporary water shortage in the town, Lord Castlerosse had evolved his own way of dealing with the emergency. It was at least practical. He had ordered forty dozen bottles of Vichy water to be warmed up so that he could shave and bathe. After an outburst of expostulations, Beaverbrook paid the bill, as he always did.

This was, in fact, a principle which Valentine insisted should be observed by everybody in Max's caravan. When anyone tried to pay a restaurant bill for a party of which Beaverbrook was a member, Valentine would stop him with a gesture of mock horror: 'Put it back in your pocket at once! *You'll spoil Max.*'

Having been persuaded that a periodic visit to Dr Dengler's sanatorium at Baden-Baden was essential to his health, and indeed to his continued existence, Valentine on one occasion made last-minute arrangements to travel there by train. On his instructions, his secretary rang up the station master at Victoria to order a sleeper for Lord Castlerosse to Baden-Baden. The station master, new to his duties, replied that, alas, it was impossible to find a sleeper for Lord Castlerosse. He was desolated but the thing simply could not be done.

Downcast but by no means defeated by this news, Castlerosse allowed the telephone to rest for a few minutes. Then he picked it up and announced that he was Lord Beaverbrook and wished a sleeper to Baden-Baden. This time, the station master was all alacrity and readiness to oblige. 'Certainly, my lord. The sleeper will be arranged.'

When Valentine turned up at Victoria, enormous, pink and obviously much in need of the healing waters of Baden-Baden, the station master doffed his top hat and saw the distinguished traveller, Lord Beaverbrook, to his carriage.

A week later, the real Lord Beaverbrook returned to Victoria from Paris. The station master, seeing him, grasped immediately what had happened. He said with a polite smile, 'That was a mighty good cure, my lord.'

When Beaverbrook took Valentine to Berlin with him as a travelling companion, he was invited to dinner by the German Chancellor, Dr Wirth. He thought that, in the circumstances, he could not solicit an invitation for Castlerosse. As a solution he said, 'Ask a few friends in for a drink.' Valentine took him at his word. From the Adlon Hotel there radiated telephone calls. Castlerosse had invited the entire British and American press corps to his suite. He entertained them there to hock at £4 a bottle.

Dining in Paris one night as Beaverbrook's guest, Valentine wished to make a telephone call. When he could not get the number, he became enraged. It was one of the misadventures in life which he found hardest to bear. His rage boiled up until, in a white heat of fury, he tore the telephone from the wall and threw it on the floor. A screen was over-turned and fell with a crash. A table was upset. The staff of the restaurant rushed about in confusion. The guests rose to their feet in anger. Lord Beaverbrook, seeing how things were going, left the table and moved quietly to the door.

Castlerosse, observing his friend's retreat, turned to the waiter. 'If there is any bill for damage,' he said amiably, 'send it to the well-behaved small man who is going out. His name is Lord Castlerosse.'

Telephones seem to have had a powerful effect on Valentine's destructive impulses. In the *Sunday Express* office he had a room next to that of the Managing Director, A. J. Russell and opposite John Gordon's. One day Gordon heard a howl and a clatter and rushed in to see what was wrong. He saw Russell cowering in one corner, Castlerosse's desk overturned, the telephone smashed on the floor and Castlerosse standing amid the debris.

'What in God's name is wrong?' he asked.

Castlerosse answered in the voice of a reasonable man who had been tried by fate beyond endurance.

'I have lost my pipe,' he explained.

However, it was not only in financial matters that Valentine was a trial to his friends. Castlerosse complained loudly about the quality of the food at Beaverbrook's table, a point on which the latter was sensitive, having no par-ticular interest in food himself.

'Max,' said Valentine on one occasion, 'this is the worst food in London.'

Beaverbrook was, pardonably, annoyed and said, 'Take Lord Castlerosse's plate away! He does not like what is on it.' Keen observers noticed, however, that the food in Beaverbrook's house improved from that moment. Before long, Valentine was able to say approvingly to a fellow-guest, 'His lordship keeps a good table.'

Claiming that the brandy which Beaverbrook served after dinner was unfit for human consumption, Castlerosse would bring his own bottle with him and put it firmly on the table. On one occasion, this cost him dear. Beaverbrook arranged for Lord Castlerosse to be called to the telephone. 'Now boys,' he said to his other guests, who included sturdy drinkers, 'help yourselves to the brandy.' The result was that when Castlerosse came back, the brandy bottle was empty. He picked it up, said nothing, but threw it into the fire.

In one respect, there was rivalry between the two men. Beaverbrook had, from time to time, a good story to tell. He told it well – better and better as time went on. Valentine, jealous of his own fame as a *raconteur*, listened with unconcealed impatience to his friend's stories, trying by all the well-tried tricks to distract the audience. Someone was asked for a light. A spoon was rattled in a cup. And so on.

On one occasion, Beaverbrook was going up the Nile in a boat with a party of friends. Valentine was one of them. Beaverbrook embarked on a rather long story and was gradually building up to the climax when Valentine yawned and broke in loudly, 'Tell me, Max, what happened to that motorcar which ran over the precipice when we were in Monte Carlo?'

Beaverbrook stopped, quite dumbfounded and very angry. 'What do you mean?' he exclaimed furiously. 'You are interrupting my story just when I was coming to the climax. What on earth has the fate of a motorcar in Monte Carlo to do with my story?'

'Nothing at all,' replied Valentine, amiably, 'but it reminded me of the time and place you told it last.'

Occasionally, Beaverbrook hired a yacht, and took a chosen troop of companions on a cruise through sunlit waters. Thus, in the mid-Thirties, he took Valentine and Brendan Bracken and some kindred spirits on a Mediterranean voyage.

On these trips, Valentine was not at his best. Sometimes

when the launch took the party ashore the sea was rough and Valentine would fly into a panic and try to clamber out of the enclosed part of the boat, as if some form of claustrophobia had overtaken him. In the same way, he became wildly alarmed if an aeroplane he was travelling in had a bumpy flight. Back on land, Valentine came into his own again.

At each port he would go ashore, returning loaded with huge parcels containing a vast amount of silk and chiffon scarves for the ladies of the party. Beaverbrook said, exasperated but amused, 'God damn him. He's doing all this with my money.' As it chanced, he had just once more paid Valentine's debts.

During the trip the yacht called at Barcelona. In the course of one adventurous evening in that port, the party visited a night club where Beaverbrook, in a spirit of mischief, incited the local hostesses to set about Valentine and Bracken.

When things grew too hot, Valentine proved equal to the situation. In those days it was his fancy to carry a swordstick, whether as a means of self-defence or as a gesture towards the picturesque past cannot be determined. Now he unsheathed this romantic weapon and flourished it in a menacing fashion.

Waving it to and fro in flashing arcs, he kept the Spanish attack at bay while the English ladies of the party took refuge under *banquettes* and Lord Beaverbrook, judging that the affair had gone far enough, fled into the night. At length the Civil Guard arrived and, after some pesetas had changed hands, peace was restored. Honour satisfied, virtue saved, the victorious Valentine put his sword back into its stick and returned in triumph to M.Y. *Alice* in the harbour, where Lord Beaverbrook awaited the return of his guests, not without some apprehension.

When it began to seem likely that another war was going to engulf Europe, Beaverbrook went to Paris and took

Valentine with him. Valentine's talents as a travelling companion were considerable; as a guide to the international situation he was not, perhaps, the most obvious choice. Commonsense and wordly wisdom are not enough to enable a man to qualify as an expert in foreign affairs. However, there he was on the Golden Arrow and, eventually, in the Ritz Hotel, scene of some of his earlier exploits.

For Beaverbrook it was a question, in particular, of knowing what the French would do if the Nazis seized Danzig from the Poles. At that time the Paris correspondent of the *Daily Express* was Geoffrey Cox,* a brilliant, level-headed journalist from New Zealand. Beaverbrook called Cox to his suite in the Ritz and explained what he had in mind.

'You will go to the Ruhr,' he said, 'and find out what the German people are feeling about the prospect of war. Lord Castlerosse will make inquiries in France and report to me about the feelings of the French.'

Cox carried out his part of the plan promptly and thoroughly. He went to the Ruhr. He saw the British consuls in various cities and met representatives of the German people. He returned to Paris to report the results of his investigation.

In the anteroom of Beaverbrook's suite he met Lord Castlerosse, pink, genial but apparently a little perturbed about the reason for their conference. This was unusual.

'Tell me, Geoffrey,' he asked, 'what really are we here for? It has slipped my memory.' Cox explained what had been in their employer's mind. 'Oh, yes,' said Castlerosse with manifest relief. 'Do you know, I had quite forgotten all about it.' But, as it turned out later, his days in Paris had not been entirely wasted.

When the consultation with Lord Beaverbrook began, Cox was asked to report first. He did so in his usual thorough and objective way. If the Ruhr was anything to go by, he said, the German people would fight to the last man and

* Now Sir Geoffrey Cox.

with enthusiasm. This was particularly true of the German working classes.

Beaverbrook listened gravely and in silence. Then he turned to Castlerosse.

'Now, Valentine,' he asked. 'What about the French? What do they feel about fighting?'

'I don't know what the French as a whole are thinking,' said Castlerosse. 'But I have studied very closely the opinion among the public on the terrace of Fouquet's restaurant and I can assure you with complete confidence that the French on Fouquet's terrace will not fight for Danzig.'

This statement, which Lord Beaverbrook did not hear with surprise or displeasure, ended the consultation on foreign affairs at that critical moment in history. In fact, whatever had been the sources of Valentine's opinion, it was a realistic summing up of French feeling at the time.

That was not Cox's first meeting with Castlerosse. Shortly before, Cox had been asked by Lord Beaverbrook to investigate the claims made on behalf of a woman faith healer currently enjoying a considerable reputation in the South of France and being given a good deal of space in the newspapers. Cox looked into the woman's claims and brought in a sceptical verdict. Soon after this, new and striking evidence of the healer's powers was produced. It seemed that, by the laying on of hands, remarkable cures had been achieved. Reports of these wonders found their way into various newspapers in France, Britain and elsewhere.

Beaverbrook, on a visit to Paris, summoned Cox to the Ritz and chided him in the presence of Castlerosse. He said that he was very depressed, as he usually was when one of his newspapers appeared to have 'missed a story'. Frowning deeply, he said, 'How unfortunate, Cox, that you allowed yourself to be scooped by our rivals on a story of this calibre.' Cox went over the reasons for his scepticism.

Beaverbrook shook his head again. He turned to Lord Castlerosse.

'What do you think, Valentine, of this woman's claim to these extraordinary powers?'

Castlerosse turned his cigar over between his fingers and looked at it judiciously.

'Well, Max', he said, 'it all depends. For example, it depends on where she laid her hands.'

From that moment onwards the conversation took on a more genial tone. It was the last they heard then or later of the pretensions of the healer or of this complaint against Geoffrey Cox for failure in his journalistic judgement. He had, thereafter, the kindliest opinion of Valentine's character and gifts as a diplomat.

16

Every man has one enemy. The clock. Some men have a second. The weighing machine. Let it be admitted that Valentine Castlerosse did not shrink from battle with the second antagonist.

On the contrary, his feats in the dining-room were remarkable. He was the only man who, in John Gordon's experience, could eat a whole ham and then a whole currant cake. His nephew, now Lord de Vesci, once saw him at the Orleans Club brush aside a helping of pigeon pie and say indignantly to the waiter, 'Bring the whole pie, you fool.'

Obviously a man could not eat on that scale without paying the price – periodic visits to Dengler's Sanatorium at Baden-Baden, from which, in 1929, he reported virtuously to Beaverbrook, 'I have lost two stone,' and in 1937 (when he weighed twenty stone) a stay at Ruthin Castle, an institution in North Wales which catered for those inclined by nature and indulgence to obesity.

At Ruthin, Valentine found himself, if not in his element, at least among his social equals, men of roughly the same rank as himself and roughly the same weight. Men, for example, like Lord Rosebery and Lord Derby. Either under the influence of the hunger which they had come to court or the anxiety which they had in common, the talk that summer at Ruthin was free and of good quality.

Thus, Lord Rosebery explained why he had come to detest

his father. And Lord Derby spoke angrily about the attacks on the royal family which the dramatist Frederick Lonsdale had made in his presence. The outcome of these was one of the best of Valentine's letters to have survived, one which shows how right Lord Beaverbrook was when he insisted that the unpublished writings of Lord Castlerosse were far better than those that reached print. The misfortune is that they have remained unpublished. It certainly makes one realize what a worthy successor to Pepys or Greville he would have made:

Ruthin Castle
Friday, June 1937

My dear Max,

Many thanks for your letter.

There is a landing ground at Cork. I will ask Arthur about it. As for other guests you shall pick them and nobody else shall be admitted.

As for being a teetotaller – it is a sad life – Up to date I have lost a stone or so and beyond an occasional dizzy spell I feel all right – but low. I could do with a drink.

You were saying that you regretted that Harry Rosebery had not done more with his life. The reason is his Father, who hunted him out of Scotland, by making life at Dalmeny so humiliating that no man could stand it.

He must have been a queer fellow, the late Lord R. He insisted on Harry leaving the Grenadiers and standing for Parliament in Edinburgh. Harry was elected. Shortly afterwards he received a letter from Campbell Bannerman asking Harry to 2nd the address.

Delighted, Harry went to his Father with the letter.

Instead of being pleased Lord R. frowned.

'If you do such a thing, you are no son of mine,' said Lord R.

'Why?' said Harry.

'Because I hate Campbell Bannerman,' said Lord R.

As Lord R. controlled the purse strings there was noth-
thing else for Harry to do – 'With my Father behind me,
tripping me up, abusing me and forbidding me to speak
to my leader, politics became an impossibility,' says
Harry.

So Harry took to cricket and sport – but even in racing
he was not allowed even to see his father's horses. Poor
Harry, his youth was unhappy.

Lord Derby is here. He tells me he saw you.

Lord D. spoke of Freddy, after dinner tonight.

'I can't stand that Freddy Lonsdale any more,' he said.
'When he moved about and saw people he was good fun
but now . . .' Lord D. made a grimace and angrily shuffled
his patience cards 'besides he did a thing I found shock-
ing. He was staying with me at Knowsley and violently
supported the Duke of Windsor in such terms as to be
disloyal to our present King.

'I said, "Any man is entitled to his own opinions, but
now we are leaving for a public ball. I hope there you
will pipe down as everybody knows you are my guest and
here in Lancashire you will cause a scandal if you reiter-
ate what you have been saying."

'Lonsdale promised that he would respect my wishes.
But damn it, five minutes after we had arrived what
should I see but Lonsdale swilling champagne and
shouting at the top of his voice that he was a repub-
lican and that the whole damned Royal family was no
good.'

There was pause. It was obvious that Lord D. was
moved for he missed 2 cards in his patience.

'Does Max see much of Freddy, I mean Lonsdale, now?'
whispered Lord Derby, looking at me sideways.

'I don't think he sees as much of him as he did,' I
replied.

Lord Derby beamed.

'I have always said that Max was a wonderful judge

of character,' he said, as he chuckled to himself.

From that we got on the subject of Hore Belisha. 'Mind you, I like him,' said Lord Derby, looking benignly at the blank wall opposite 'and in many ways I admire him. I expect he will do a great deal better at the War Office than Duff did. I expect you like Duff as much as I do ' . . . there was a pause as he glanced at the King of Spades. 'What do you think is the matter with Duff? The generals did not really cotton to him at the War Office, they said he did not put their case properly to the Cabinet. Then of course when I filled the Free Trade Hall for him to make a recruiting speech, he shocked everybody by a violent attack on the Bishops . . .'

'You say he drinks too much brandy' – I hadn't, in fact, spoken.

'But what about Belisha,' I said.

'Oh yes,' said Lord Derby, 'you hear him abused, but you never hear me say a word against him. There was one incident. You remember the new Liverpool-Manchester road and tunnel. Oliver was to open that. His name was actually carved into the stone.

'The King and Queen performed the ceremony and had specially asked for Oliver. Then the reshuffle took place and H.B. came to the Ministry of Transport. This little Jew, INSISTED, yes INSISTED on being Minister in waiting. Not only that but wrote and said he presumed he was invited to Knowsley – which I thought pretty good cheek.'

'Did you refuse?' I said.

'Oh no!' replied Lord Derby, 'and do you know that from Knowsley he carried on a propaganda of self-glorification in the newspapers.'

I was so horrified that I did not know what to say but looked at the table next to Lord Derby's bed and saw 2 books on horse trading, Ruff's guide to the Turf, a detective story and a prayer book.

Harry at this juncture came in and the subject turned on Lord Dudley.

'Eric's grandfather was a changeling,' said Lord Derby. 'So I have heard,' said Harry. 'It happened like this,' continued Lord Derby taking no notice of the interruption. 'Lady Dudley was in Rome. She wanted a son. A daughter was born; so a swop was effected. Mildred Meux whenever she sees Bobby Ward always pretends to play a barrel organ. I don't think he likes it.'

But here I am running on and boring you.

I will write to you again. I propose to return Sunday night, that is Sunday week. I suppose you know why Lord Derby could never understand Baldwin? 'After all I never expected to be treated like that' – about the resignation and all that.

I hope all goes well

Yrs ever Valentine

In 1939 Valentine took seriously ill while lunching at Claridges. Doctors, headed by Dr Wilson,* nurses, servants, chauffeur, secretary, were in attendance; friends hovered solicitously. A suite in Claridges was the centre of these happenings. There were nights when Dr Wilson slept on the field of battle and hardly a morning passed but Welsh, the servant, drew up a list of callers for his master to read, and correct the spelling.

Valentine's ideas of conduct suitable to one who was very ill were whimsical. A nurse complained that one whose liver, heart and breathing were gravely impaired and who had a high temperature ought not to stand naked in front of an open window practising golf swings.

A day came when Lord Beaverbrook (who was, incidentally, paying all the costs of this circus, plus an accumulation of the invalid's debts amounting to £1,500) decided that the twin causes of health and economy would be served if Lord

* Later Lord Moran.

Castlerossse were transferred to the London Clinic. There discipline could be imposed, visitors could be banned and food be rationed.

And so it was, except that many charming friends of the sick man broke through the cordon in the guise of faith healers. Unsuspected by Dr Wilson, Valentine had become a convinced believer in this kind of therapy, especially when it was practised by pretty and amusing young women of his acquaintance.

One exceptionally attentive healer was Leonora Corbett, a beautiful actress of the time who had become a close friend of Valentine's after the divorce from Doris. He claimed that she had rekindled in him his old love for the theatre.

There was another problem. The standard of cooking at the Clinic fell far below his lordship's expectations. Accordingly, meals were brought in from Claridges by Claridges' waiters. Beaverbrook, paying a visit to the invalid one day, shared a lift at the Clinic with one of those food convoys. He was interested and puzzled and, when he had discovered what was going on, appropriately indignant. Valentine's bed, too, had been brought over from Claridges.

All was not given over to frivolity. Lady Kenmare came to see her prodigal. A priest came with her. Thereupon Valentine sent a message to the *Cork Examiner* to inform the anxious population of southern Ireland that he had received the last rites of the Church. Beaverbrook intercepted the telegram which, with his trained insight into Valentine's mind, he thought was simply a stratagem to persuade the most importunate creditors to hold their hands.

Castlerosse wrote to correct any misapprehension of this kind, and to explain why he was anxious that the telegram had been stopped. After all, it would be well enough known in Ireland that it had been sent.

'Down home,' he told Lord Beaverbrook, ' people take

the last Sacrament devilish seriously. I was frightened they might think I was putting a swift one over on them.'

He went on to talk about the golf course he was planning to build at Killarney, and the necessity there was that he should supervise it in person.

'On the point out in the lake, in the centre of the course there is a cottage surrounded by beautiful trees. You ought to go and see it. Fly over one day or take a liner to Cork. I think it is where the angels came to rest . . . If you like it, I'll give it to you.'

But his health worried him more than he was ready to admit, except to his most intimate friends.

'This I would like to know. Am I going to die slowly or swiftly? Is my heart all bust up? I cannot clean my teeth without the damned thing giving an imitation of an airplane engine. Doctors won't tell . . . Death means nothing to me. The only living thing I possess is a dog and she is a bitch.'

Then he hoped that he could write his own obituary – 'It would be a change to write about something I know.' Six weeks later, the picture was different. Lord Castlerosse had recovered enough to convalesce in Paris and resume working on 'The Londoner's Log'. Alas, a year later he was back in Ruthin Castle once more, having put on five stone in a year.

When the Second World War came and brought with it restrictions in food, it faced Valentine with problems which he surmounted in his own way. He stayed for a time with Lord Beaverbrook at Cherkley. Every morning after breakfast, he went up to London. He had an early luncheon at White's Club, and went on to luncheon at the St James's. In due course, he returned to White's where he appeased his hunger with an early dinner. He had to watch the clock, though, so that he could be back at Cherkley in time for dinner at Lord Beaverbrook's frugal but sufficient table. Nobody is so resourceful as a hungry man with a keen appetite.

Had Castlerosse been in Paris during the Siege he would certainly have eaten the elephant in the zoo.

Like many another man, Castlerosse's attachment to the place of his upbringing grew stronger as the years passed. This process was helped, of course, by the unhappiness of his marriage. He was estranged and, finally, divorced from his wife. They had no children. His health worried him, and with good reason. The high spirits remained but somehow the real zest had gone.

And he shrank, as most men of his generation did, from the prospect of another war. He could see that it was likely to come – that it was, perhaps, inevitable. But that did not make it any less repugnant. As Britain became more and more powerfully drawn into the European storm, Castlerosse thought more and more about Ireland. Over there was Killarney. There was his home. And as it chanced there was something useful and constructive which he could do better than anyone else. Something which involved Killarney.

He was, moreover, increasingly out of touch with his friend, Beaverbrook, more and more disenchanted with journalism. 'The Londoner's Log' no longer had its former place in the world. It had begun to bore its writer. But in Ireland . . . Valentine had an idea about Ireland which excited him and finally obsessed him.

It is curious that what in the end gave him the most satisfaction in life was an idea about golf. But so it was. Valentine was an extraordinarily good golfer who, but for a failure in temperament, would certainly have got his blue for Cambridge University, for which, in fact, he played once or twice. But his headstrong nature, his passionate urge to avenge himself on his clubs for any momentary weakness in his play, his insistence that he should be accompanied on a round by a servant bearing a jug of whisky from which, from time to time, he would fill a tumbler and instantly empty it – all these eccentricities made him the terror of golf club secretaries over the breadth of south-eastern

England. Even so, he was probably the best golfer who ever played the game without a right elbow.

His misadventures on the course were legendary. When he was playing in the competition for the President's Putter at Deal, he had the misfortune to hit a ball into a famous and formidable bunker. The ball, when he came to examine it, was almost buried in sand. A crowd gathered round to see how the famous Lord Castlerosse would deal with the emergency. They saw him raise his eyes to heaven. They heard his pious supplication. 'Oh, God, come down and help me with this shot. And don't send Jesus . . . This is no job for a boy.'

Whether as a result of this prayer or not, Valentine's shot was successful. His ball was lifted clear out of the sand. And Valentine poured himself a drink from his celebrated jug of whisky.

Later on, when he came to design his own golf course, he saw to it that there was no need for him to be accompanied on a round by a bearer of whisky. He made other arrangements.

One day, he wrote that there were two hundred acres of land on the lakeshore at Killarney which the Almighty had designed to be the site of a golf course. The land, as it chanced, was Kenmare property, known in the estate records as the Western Demesne. As time went on, the idea of the golf course germinated and grew more precise. He took into his confidence his friend Henry Longhurst, who was not only a fellow journalist but the best golfing writer of the day. Longhurst was invited to Killarney where Valentine, standing at Mahoney's Point, on the margin of the lake, asked Longhurst, 'Do you think that this would make a lovely golf course?'

'The loveliest in the world,' replied Longhurst.

Valentine pointed at the ground and said, 'Here will be the first tee.' And there today is, indeed, the first tee of the magnificent golf course which was, to Valentine at least, the dearest and most abiding of his brainchildren. On the day that he expounded his ideas to Longhurst, there was nothing at Mahoney's Point except a boatman's cottage, which has since vanished to be replaced by a fine clubhouse, and a little avenue of trees leading to the water's edge. The avenue can still be seen.

For Longhurst there followed days in which he was a surprised witness of Valentine's enthusiasm as a stalker. A procession would be formed when the keeper's report had been heard. Lord Castlerosse, Mr Longhurst, a keeper, another keeper carrying rifles and telescopes, finally, but not least important, a man bearing a pail with ice for his lordship's whisky and soda. When at length the most favourable firing point had been selected, Longhurst would be sent off to carry out an encircling movement. He would return to find that Castlerosse had killed a fine stag without moving a yard and was enjoying his first whisky and soda of the day.

At the end of the stay, Longhurst had acquired a considerable respect for his host's marksmanship. In fact, Valentine's prowess with a gun is still legendary in Co. Kerry. He thought nothing of rising at half past five in the morning, killing a stag and eating its liver fresh for breakfast. He waged a constant war against the deer of Killarney maintaining, and with justice, that they were far too numerous and did far too much damage.

Valentine's idea was that the Killarney Golf Course should, quite simply, be the best and the most beautiful in the world. To achieve this, he employed the best available professional talent, plus of course his own vision and the golfing genius of Henry Longhurst.

Reginald Purbrick, a rich Conservative MP, was brought in to lend financial support.

At that time, the world's leading architect of golf courses was Sir Guy Campbell. Valentine brought Campbell to Killarney and walked over the ground with him day after day during the months of 1938 and 1939, marking out the sites of tees, greens, and bunkers with bamboo poles. When the time came to translate plans into the realities of turf and sand, Valentine introduced a Scotsman named Hamilton White to carry out the practical work of earth-moving, draining and sowing. The work was more complicated than usual. Valentine insisted that from every green there should be a view of the lake.

Then he had the poetic notion that each hole would be associated with a different kind or colour of shrub or heather. To carry out the scheme, Valentine took counsel with Mr W. M. Campbell, the Curator at Kew. ' I am determined,' he said, ' to call on the paintbox of Heaven and draw a panorama of 150 acres in massed colours. The thing is to be as loud and vulgar as God will let you . . . I am having three banks of one acre each of wild native flowers, then an Australian bank and also a New Zealand bank.' The only trouble came from the sheep which were used to crop the grass and had a partiality for shrubs. Still, the idea has in general survived, as a visit to Killarney will show.

Then there was the question of refreshment for the thirsty golfer. Valentine set up a series of huts about the course, of which he had the key. In each hut was a bottle of whisky.

The question of labour arose and was quickly settled. Valentine took the advice of the Irish Ministry of Agriculture. He was told that there was no real problem. All the local farmers' sons spent the winter in the workhouse where they were fed but were given no money. If he fed them better than the workhouse, he could have their labour free of payment.

More serious was the question of the Church, which must give its blessing if the scheme was to come to anything. Valentine invited the Cardinal Archbishop to dinner at Killarney. His Eminence, after being assured that the golf course would bring no loose women to the district, agreed that it might be created. And so Valentine's proposal went forward with the blessing of the Church.

In 1938, before the course was completed, Valentine wrote, 'Next year, unless an evil fate overtakes us, the Killarney Golf Course will be one of the wonders of the world but it will be a little more than merely a golf playing ground.'

What he had in mind was that, in a changing world, with Shannon Airport about to develop as a main junction of air traffic, there would be a vast influx of tourists from America. A golf course of international fame at Killarney would persuade many of them to make something more than a brief pause in Ireland.

Alas, though, an evil fate did ' overtake us '. One Sunday in October 1939, the Bishop of Kerry blessed the course and Castlerosse, who had come over from England for the event, drove from the first tee. He topped the ball, which in the circumstances seemed an appropriate commentary on the situation. For the war, which he had foreseen and detested, had come and, it seemed, that all his hopes for Killarney were laid in ruins. He was in a state of deep depression.

Next day he heard from Beaverbrook, then on his way home from the United States, that he would drop in and inspect the golf course. The news cheered Valentine up enormously. 'You are the first,' he told his friend, 'who has ever ordered the gates of hell to be closed and propped open the gates of heaven.' His first act on receiving Beaverbrook's message was to enter the clubhouse and order drinks all round.

On the day the second war came and all the pessimists were proved right, Valentine was staying at his cottage at Walton Heath. He wrote an article which appeared the following morning, Monday 4 September 1939, in the *Daily Express*. It is a good example of his writing when he was at the top of his form, moved by a great occasion, and able in a few crisp sentences to convey a scene, an atmosphere, a feeling. It opened like this:

It must have been round about half past eleven o'clock in the morning and Walton Heath was looking its best. The sun was shining. The turf was green and springy.

A groom had just passed riding a thoroughbred horse, which is ever cheery to see.

The little larks were flying joyfully in the sky. A man in a green shirt had hit a good drive off the fourteenth tee when suddenly we heard a distant sound.

It sounded as if all the banshees of the world had joined together to give voice to a united wail.

'That must be war,' I said to Captain Wardell.

Captain Wardell did not reply. He was too busy looking for his pipe, which he did not know then was reposing on his dressing-table.

After a while, when he had made perfectly certain that the search would be fruitless, Captain Wardell turned to me and said: 'Yes without doubt war has been declared and we had better make up our minds here and now that this will alter everything.'

And so, for the first time, the word 'banshee' was used in describing the sound of the air-raid warning. Later, Churchill was to make the word his own.

In his article Castlerosse went on to give the British people some advice, which they probably did not need to hear, about how they should behave in the altered world which had suddenly sprung up about them:

Don't go about the countryside boasting as to what you are going to do with the Germans.

Swashbuckling is not native to the British character and it becomes us ill.

Don't vent your wrath on some unfortunate individual,

for those who are responsible for this war are not in England today.

Likewise, if a man says something which displeases you, don't lose your temper.

If you cannot trust yourself not to do so, walk away. Otherwise take a mental pledge of silence.

In fact, there was no real place for Valentine in the grim wartime Britain which was born on that September morning in 1939. He could not fight. His journalism was out of key. The restrictions, the austerity, the need for discipline – these would have been irritating in any case. But, for him as for others of his generation, they were all happening for the second time.

In these circumstances, was it surprising that Ireland made an ever stronger appeal? Above all, there was the Golf Course, that dream become reality, which he could refine and beautify. It was, however, not the only interest in his life, as it turned out.

One day in 1940 Carol Reed, the film director, discussed with Robert Kane of Twentieth Century Fox the problems concerning a film of *Rob Roy* which they were planning to make. There were practical difficulties. How, they wondered, was the film to be made on location in Scotland in wartime conditions? Apart from anything else, there was the blackout.

In the course of the discussion, Kane suggested that the scenery in Ireland was very like that of Scotland. He mentioned a friend of his, Lord Castlerosse, who could speak with more authority on this. As a sequel to this conversation, Reed was introduced to Castlerosse. He found the Irishman obsessed with the idea of finding employment for the people of his part of Ireland, Killarney. At that time, this was the over-riding interest in Castlerosse's life.

He invited Reed over to stay with him at Killarney, where he was living in the converted stables of the old mansion his grandfather had built in the far-off days of Queen Victoria. Reed was delighted with his host's conversation and fascinated by the atmosphere of the place. Castlerosse took him over the roofless, grassgrown ruins of the house in which he had been brought up. How it had come to be burned down was, according to his story, a mystery. And he told Reed the legend of the chambermaid who on her deathbed had confessed that she had been reading in bed by candle-light when the wind blew a curtain across the flame and she had been too frightened to confess . . .

He took Reed for walks on the mountains, he himself walking with his tall, knotted cherrywood staff. One day a stag was shot. On another an old man standing outside a cottage brought his grandchild forward and, with a great show of deference, presented the child to Castlerosse, who asked the old man to cut a stick for Reed from the cherry tree growing outside his cottage. Reed has it to this day.

The two were rowed on the lake by eight retainers, one of whom told Reed stories about the fairies who could be seen at times on various hills. Castlerosse, who had warned Reed that he must not on any account appear to be amused by these tales, listened to them with every sign of surprise and seriousness, although no doubt he had heard them many times before.

Reed agreed that Killarney would make a perfect setting for the *Rob Roy* film – a project which, in fact, was finally abandoned when the German breakthrough in the West occurred. About that time, Valentine was once more anxious about his weight. On 21 April 1940 he reported to Beaverbrook from Ruthin, ' I have put on about five stone in one year. I propose to take it off in two attacks.' On 2 May, ' I have lost 17 lb. The golf course is a startling success.' On 23 May, writing from Kenmare House, ' I have lost two stone. The IRA are expected to rise . . .' His association with Carol Reed did not end with the frustrated *Rob Roy* venture. The two men had formed a liking for one another, and Valentine had become fascinated with the movie business. They met in London later on at a time when Reed was making *Kipps* at Shepherds Bush. He persuaded Castlerosse to appear in the film as an irascible fat man sitting in a bath chair on the front at Brighton. It was not a difficult part and Castlerosse played it with conviction.

One day, when they were having luncheon in Claridges, Valentine spilt some port on the tablecloth. ' If that had happened to William Pitt,' he said, ' it would have driven him mad.' He went on to expatiate on Pitt's life and character, his weakness for port, his relations with his father and so forth.

From this talk there emerged the germ of the film *The Young Mr Pitt*, for the making of which Valentine was engaged as an adviser. He took the job very seriously, calling for Reed with his car every morning just before nine and driving with him down to the studios. There he would loosen his tie, take off his coat and sit down, serious, busy and completely professional, to tackle the job of script writing.

He worked hard, providing a flow of ideas and a profusion of suggested dialogue to the director. In all, he impressed everybody with his dedication to the task. It is not at all impossible that, had it not been for the war and, later, the sudden collapse of his health, Castlerosse would have become a figure in the movie business.

Now that journalism was coming to an end for him, he was tempted to find a fresh outlet there for his talents. Films might have been the answer to his quest. What is certain is that *The Young Mr Pitt*, in which Robert Donat played the title role, was completed and was a success with the public.

But it was in Ireland rather than in the shadow of Shepherds Bush that Valentine's real interests were centred by that time. Across the vast demesne of Killarney he would roam, pipe in mouth, brows knit in profound thought and wearing one of his collection of resplendent plus-four suits, perhaps the rainbow-coloured tweed, perhaps the pink. His particular anxiety at that time was to plant a clump of hydrangeas at a strategic point on the course. He devoted a great deal of thought to the problem of finding the right site first.

And in south-west Ireland there was a sufficiency of people to whom he could talk, among them Colonel Knowles and his wife who spent every summer at Reen-na Furraha, Sneem, at the mouth of Kenmare River, about thirty miles away. There were young people; stalking expeditions on the mountain tracks above Killarney, after Valentine's old enemies, the deer; picnics; and at the end of the day vast family dinner parties in Killarney House, where the atmosphere was warm and friendly most of the time, and Valentine presided at the head of the table.

17

Meanwhile Doris had gone to America. Valentine had divorced her in July 1938 after years of estrangement and separation. He professed publicly to be delighted with what he said was a deliverance.

Doris had lost her looks, so he said – 'I caught sight of her the other day. I bowed politely. The truth is, I thought it was her mother.' To others, however, Doris was still attractive.

Such a continued, tortured interest in the woman to whom he had been married suggested that Valentine's parting from Doris was by no means the happy release that he pretended it was. It was something far more complex.

After several associations, Doris had formed a friendship with a rich American woman, Mrs Margaret Flick Hoffman, who gave her the Palazzo Venier dei Leone on the Grand Canal in Venice. The garden of this palazzo is beautiful but melancholy; today, the house contains the Guggenheim collection of modern pictures.

Doris squandered a great deal of Mrs Hoffman's money on the decoration of the establishment, which she claimed was the only house in Venice in which every bedroom had its own bathroom. Before long, Doris was one of the celebrities of the city, with her own gondola and liveried gondoliers. Her behaviour was, at times, as generous and even uninhibited as was to be expected.

One night, not long before the war, she gave a party at the palazzo the fame of which lingers on. A dance floor was built in the garden. The lights were reflected on the surface of the canal. The Venetian aristocracy were out in strength. Prince Philip, who was staying in the city with his uncle, Prince Christopher of Greece, was also present. It was a memorable rout.

Upon this carefree existence, war fell like a leaden fist.

Doris felt that Britain in the conditions that were likely to prevail during a war was not for her. She had much the same repugnance for it as had her former husband. In any case, America and kindly Mrs Hoffman offered an easier alternative. Or so it seemed. Mrs Hoffman could promise her friend hospitality both in New York and in the house her father, a rich manufacturer, owned at Lennox, Pennsylvania. Accordingly, one day Doris and her Rolls Royce left by ship for New York.

She remained in the United States until late in 1942. Then one day she flew back. For this event, which could have been foreseen, there was a variety of motives. Her friendship with Mrs Hoffman was not what it had been. And, now that the United States was in the war, Doris felt as out of place there as she had done in Britain. It seemed that not only London but New York – the world! – was no longer recognizable as that in which she had flourished.

She wrote to her brother in England one day in May 1942, 'I have been trying to get home but it seems impossible. I am so homesick and miserable being away from England.'

There was, too, a third circumstance which played an important part in her thoughts at that time.

A few years before, in Maxine Elliott's splendid villa near Cannes, Château de l'Horizon, she had met Winston Churchill. Maxine Elliott was one of the most extraordinary characters of an age of garish adventure. She had been born in 1871 as Jessica Dermot, one of the two daughters of an Irish-American Maine sea captain. 'Divinely tall, divinely dark', she survived a convent education to become a highly successful actress, and had made two disastrous marriages to alcoholics.

But she had a loyal friend, Pierpont Morgan, the banker, to whose financial advice she listened, profitably.* Maxine came to England, conquered Society which was easy enough to a rich, beautiful, unattached American woman and became – as pretty women did at that time – a friend of King Edward VII. She had a suite in her country house in Hertfordshire which she called 'The King's Suite'.

In her fine villa on the Riviera, Maxine Elliott gave hospitality to a wide circle of English guests, among whom was Winston Churchill, whose mother had, like herself, been united by a close bond of friendship with the late King Edward.

When Winston met Doris Castlerosse there she had appealed to him as an artist. He thought that she would make a delightful subject for one of his paintings. So Doris had sat for her portrait by Churchill and during the sittings had fascinated him with her beauty, intelligence, frankness and humour. He responded to her appeal with all the strength of his romantic nature.

They were, no doubt, a strangely assorted pair, the elder statesman who seemed at that time to be barred for ever from a return to the political heights and the beautiful divorcee with the adventurous life and the brilliant mind. But they had things in common – disappointment, intelligence, and the appreciation by each that the other was an exceptional person. Romantic friendship? Or intellectual affinity? Whatever name should be given to the relationship it is certain that it was all the more charming because it was, for each, a surprise.

After their first encounter at Maxine Elliott's villa, where

* When she died in 1940, she was worth £326,000.

Churchill was a frequent visitor when Parliament was not sitting, they met from time to time in London. In all, Churchill painted three portraits of Doris.

One day at Cannes, during a sitting for one of the portraits, Winston's son Randolph had burst in on the artist and his model. He had used a common English swear word. His father had rebuked the young man in the sharpest terms: ' Wash out your mouth, my boy, after using such words in a lady's hearing.' Randolph had apologized and, knowing Doris's command of the more pungent levels of the vernacular, had departed to share with others the full comedy of the situation.

It is said that Randolph wished greatly – like so many other young men – to sleep with Doris. Some say he succeeded in this ambition. As Doris told the story, however, she had barred him from her bed on the ground that he smelt of castor oil. It was an unusual reason. But then, it was an unusual event.

In the early weeks of 1942, Winston was paying the first of his historic wartime visits to Washington. According to the story as Doris told it, Churchill invited her to a private dinner party in a Washington hotel. His motives were, it seems, twofold. He had heard – falsely – that she had been decrying the Allied cause among her friends in the United States and wished to stop it. To make certain of that he argued it was obviously advisable that Doris should come back to Britain without delay.

It was possible, too, and in the circumstances highly likely, that his portraits of Doris, which were by this time stored in New York, might fall into the hands of an American magazine publisher who could use them to damage the reputation of Britain's war leader. It was important to avert this danger, especially at a moment when Churchill's prestige was so vital a factor in Anglo-American relations.

The simplest plan would be for Churchill or a trusted friend to buy the pictures back from Doris. It seems, how-

ever, that this project did not succeed, although there is some
doubt about the way in which matters developed.

But it can be said that, soon after the Churchill visit to
Washington, Doris opened her campaign to return to
England. She used influence with President Roosevelt,
through Harry Hopkins. She did not hesitate to invoke the
name of Winston Churchill. And eventually, by one method
or another, she obtained a priority air passage to England,
something which, in those days, was more precious than
gold.

She sent Valentine a cable to herald her arrival. This was
a severe test of his character, his generosity and his commonsense. He was being asked to meet the wife from whom he
had parted and with whom he was not going to live again.
Putting the past aside, he met Doris at Waterloo station.
There he stood, a massive, sombre figure in the blackout.

He had, in fact, never put her out of his thoughts. He had
even written to her in New York urging her to come back.
On several occasions at that time he spoke of her to Carol
Reed. For instance, noticing some yellow daffodils in a flower
vase, he remarked to Reed, who had never met Doris, ' Ah,
how pretty they are. Doris always liked yellow.'

Now he found her much changed from the witty, sharp-
tongued woman he had known so well and quarrelled with
so bitterly. That he would not re-marry her, she had been
told. She had suggested it and he had rejected it, firmly
enough but not perhaps decisively. What then did she – or
he – expect from the meeting?

Some miracle, perhaps, obliterating the years and the
quarrels? If that was so, it did not occur, although afterwards Doris confided to a trusted friend her belief that
Valentine would change his mind and re-marry her. She
detected signs of wavering in him and she was, be it remembered, a woman of great experience in the ways of men.

They dined together at the Dorchester as well as wartime
diners could, which – Valentine being what he was – was

probably not too austerely. And, at the end of dinner, they parted.

Doris was left to the grim novelties of the London night in the depths of war. It was all so different from the town she had known, the town to which she thought she was returning, to open up the house she owned in Berkeley Square, to bring back the furniture she had stored in the country, to assemble once more the cheerful companions of the past.

As for the portraits of her by Winston Churchill she had brought them to the Dorchester with her. They would make distinguished ornaments on the walls in Berkeley Square.

But the pictures remained in their wrappings. The companions were fled, scattered by war across the world, in regiments, ships, factories, offices, canteens. Outside, the streets of London lay under the spell of the blackout. Far away, a siren sounded. And suddenly the big naval anti-aircraft guns in Hyde Park blurted out, shaking the room and making the glasses on the tray tremble.

It was the kind of night which millions of people in England had come to take completely for granted. But it was strange and alarming to Doris.

In a week or so she would be able to take it more calmly. But in the meantime in the jar on the table at her bedside were the sleeping tablets a doctor had given her and, as it turned out, Doris would not be granted the time needed to steady her nerves.

It was the beginning of the era of nylon stockings, which were still almost unobtainable in England. Doris telephoned a woman friend from the old days and offered to send her some. The friend was very brusque with her.

' You have behaved too badly,' she said, ' deserting Britain at a time like this.'

' What am I supposed to do ?' Doris asked.

' You can come and help me with my war work,' said the friend.

Some days later, she ran into one of those wartime problems which afflicted newcomers who did not realize how grim were the bureaucratic controls which necessity had imposed on the nation. She had pawned some jewels in New York, and now she sent a cable to New York, asking what had happened to the money.

In her innocence, she did not understand that every telegram leaving the country was read by the censors. Nor did it occur to her that, as it was phrased, her telegram appeared to refer to an illegal sale of jewellery in New York.

When detectives arrived at the hotel to question her, she gave candid replies to all the questions they asked. But she was worried by this incident in the strange, war-centred and seemingly hostile England to which she had returned. She was tough and experienced – a woman of the world. But she was alone, and this was not the world she had known.

Then, in the corridor of the hotel, she encountered the Duke of Marlborough, who made a contemptuous remark about people who deserted their country in wartime. In Doris's depressed state this made a deeper impression on her than it would normally have done.

Not long afterwards she was found in her room in the Dorchester, unconscious. She was taken to St Mary's Hospital where, after a few days, she died of an overdose of sleeping pills.

Valentine, deeply distressed, visited her often in hospital and carried the news of her death to Beaverbrook.

The coroner's verdict was death from barbiturate acid poisoning, ' the drug being self-administered in circumstances not fully disclosed by the evidence '.

With this open verdict, the death of Doris could be left to the opinion of her friends. The most perceptive of them did not believe that she had taken her life. She was in a nervous state, no doubt; she was depressed. But she was not, they thought, the kind of woman to commit suicide.

It had been an accident, they believed. And with the greater knowledge we have of the confused mental state that a mixture of sleeping pills and drink can induce – ' Have I taken my pills? I can't remember ' – this opinion should now prevail.

Valentine thought otherwise. He believed in the suicide theory and, as could be expected from a man of his nature, blamed himself extravagantly for the tragedy. The friend who had spoken to her so brusquely about the nylons did the same. Had she contributed to pushing Doris over the edge? Neither knew about the affair of the jewellery. Neither knew then about the Duke of Marlborough.

By her will, made in New York a year before, Doris left the proceeds of her motorcars and jewellery to her brother's children. The house in Berkeley Square, the palazzo on the Grand Canal, Venice, and the furniture which had been in the Berkeley Square house and was now stored in the country went to Mrs Hoffman on condition that she paid Doris's debts, failing which they were to go to her brother's children. The residue went to her brother.

Shaken by the tragedy, full of misery and self-accusation – above all, the accusation that he had failed to re-marry Doris as in the end she had wished – Valentine fled from Cherkley, where he had been staying with Beaverbrook. Before going he wrote a poignant note to his friend:

I thought I would hurry away because, anyway for the moment, I find company a strain. The clown laughs and jokes but there is no mirth in him. Wish I do not to parade the feelings in me but they are deep and cumulative. Why it must be for twenty years that I have laughed with people and slept with despair.

You know, these situations do not respond to reason. There is no logic in love. I loved Doris with a folly and futility that passes belief. Without doubt she treated me ill, as badly maybe as a woman ever treated a man – yet the argument to me bears no strength for, if a man is not full and generous in forgiveness, there can be no place among the angels for him . . .

How was it, with my past and with the knowledge that I had so painfully acquired, that I did not see that a crisis had arisen? I could have lifted Doris up, given her hope, but I did not. I let her die and all because for once I was going to be wise . . . Anyway, reason is a bare skeleton. There is but one tremendous force in the world and it is love – and I loved Doris . . .

And with that avowal – for the letter goes on and on in anguished self-tormentings – a line may be drawn beneath the story of Doris Delavigne, the beautiful, generous, and wayward, and of the foolish, big-hearted, self-dramatizing man who had married her so disastrously for them both and who, had she lived, would probably have married her again.

Let the last word be spoken by a wiser man. 'There is a land of the living and a land of the dead,' says Thornton Wilder, 'and the bridge is love, the only survival, the only meaning.'

18

Three weeks after writing that letter to Lord Beaverbrook, Valentine married for the second time. The proximity of the two events is proof – of what? The insincerity of the writer? The fickleness of human affection? Or, simply, that life can, and sometimes must, be lived on more levels than one. There can be no mistaking the note of human anguish in the letter, but it was anguish for a past that was irrevocably over and was all the more pitiable for that reason.

Ahead lay a new life, and Valentine was not the man to forgo it. He married an Australian lady, Enid, Lady Furness, in Brompton Oratory. The bride and bridegroom had known one another since the First World War, when Lady Furness was a young Australian widow living in Paris.

The church was full of his friends for the wedding, a picturesque gathering. His nephew, Lord de Vesci, sat between Mr Hore Belisha, former Minister of War, and Steve Donoghue, the jockey. Hannen Swaffer, a well-known journalist of the time, looked with a jaundiced eye on the scene which he said took place ' in a night club setting for all the titled crooks and rogues in London were there '. Captain Wardell collected subscriptions from Valentine's friends for a wedding present – glass from Fortnum and Mason. The subscribers were Lords Rosebery, Portal, McGowan, Ashfield, Brownlow, Queensberry, Kemsley, Camrose and Cranbourne, Sir Humphrey de Trafford, Sir Robert Bruce Lockhart, Wing

Commander Max Aitken, Mr James Stuart, MP, Mr J. D. Greenway, Mr Jack Solomon, and Captain Wardell.

After the wedding, the bride and bridegroom left for a holiday at Killarney. They had not been long back in London staying at the bride's house, 3 Lees Place, when it was found that a landmine had been dropped on the roof and failed to explode. Valentine begged his wife to leave the place. When she refused, he retreated in some annoyance to a room in Claridges. Later they returned to Kerry, where they entertained a large circle of friends living in that part of Ireland. On those occasions Valentine recovered his old genial, exuberant form, sitting opposite his wife in the dining-room eating heartily and drinking from an enormous glass.

He would invite each member of the party to give an account of his day, and then repeat the story in his own way, making it sound ten times as amusing as the original version. The arts of the writer of 'Londoner's Log' lived on.

Most of the time, he was an easy and entertaining host. If Black Care sat behind the horseman, he rarely showed it. As for the gloomy warnings of the doctors – 'Cut down your eating and drinking, or die' – it was as if they had never reached his ear. His disapproval could, however, be devastating.

Appropriately enough, one of the most monumental of his outbursts concerned the Irish Guards. One schoolboy guest had the impudence to suggest that the Irish Guards were not so particular as some other regiments in the recruits they accepted. A terrible hush fell on the room. The hapless young man had hit upon the one subject on which Valentine felt with the passion of an enraged patriot.

His breathing became agitated; the colour in his cheeks came and went. With a gasp, he asked the ladies to leave the room. They did so in a hurry. At their heels followed the men, all except the culprit, who stayed behind to receive a brief but impassioned discourse on military history and was not seen for the rest of the evening. But if sometimes the *bonhomie* was overclouded, the wit was as sharp as ever.

On some evenings Valentine would propose a game of bridge. Then the warier of his guests would lose no time about vanishing, for they had discovered that Valentine's ideas about bridge were governed by a strange, aberrant logic. If, for example, he discovered in his own hand that he held no card higher than a nine, he leapt to the conclusion that his partner must, on the law of averages, hold cards of surpassing excellence. His eyes gleaming with amusement and cupidity at the thought of the killing he was about to make, he would call something extravagant, say a little slam.

He bred and loved Shetland collie dogs and one dog, Rory, a cross between a black Labrador and a Chow, which became a legend in that part of Ireland. He travelled the roads and swam the rivers and the sea. Swimming, he looked like a seal and ate raw fish as they did. Nobody could catch him. Rory was known as the Gom-dog (fool dog) and outlived his breeder for years.

One beautiful Sunday in September 1943, Valentine sent a message to his friends, the Knowleses, inviting them to stay next day at Killarney on their way through to Listowel. But before she could contact him, next day, Mrs Knowles received a different message.

On that day, Valentine (whose wife Enid had left for England with her sons a few days before) was cutting roses in the garden at Killarney. He ordered his car to be brought round. Then he went to his room. He pressed the electric bell to call his servant. The bell went on ringing. When the servant arrived he found him unconscious. He died soon after.

Henry Longhurst, granted leave from the Army to visit his friend Lord Castlerosse, rang Killarney from his hotel in Dublin and asked for Valentine. A weeping servant said that he was dead. In the background, Longhurst thought he could hear the sounds of an Irish wake.

After an interval, necessary at that time because of transport difficulties, Valentine's friends were assembled and the funeral took place in St Mary's Cathedral at Killarney on the Friday after his death. It was a beautiful September day, warm and sunny. Killarney looked at its best for the man who had planned to do so much for it. Seven thousand people watched the cortège pass on the way to the Cathedral.

At the Requiem Mass, as the coffin was carried on the shoulders of family retainers to be placed in the open vault in the Kenmare Chapel, Valentine's widow, his brother Gerald, now the Earl, and his closer friends gathered round for the final blessing. What followed was unexpected.

As the bearers lowered their heavy burden towards the vault, it plunged forward with uncontrollable speed towards the depths below. Consternation! An appalling interruption in the solemnity of the moment.

Yet, as it seemed to the fancy of more than one member of the grief-stricken congregation, there was high up in the Gothic vault of the Church, the faint echo of high-pitched, derisive laughter. And the momentary vision of a jovial, rubicund man in rainbow-coloured tweed, or a white waistcoat, black jacket and slippers embroidered with crossed Cs. The incident, at once absurd, painful and poignant, was one which would have been relished to the full by the great jester to whom at that moment his friends were saying farewell.

They were saying farewell, as they probably knew, to a wonderful, baroque personality, one who was ampler and stranger than anything he had done in life. Yet in his way he had lived well, true to an inner light of wilfulness and extravagance. His own opinion was that he had wasted his life. Did he really think so, or was this just one of the many shafts of self-accusation he aimed, half-seriously, at himself? More important, had he really made a mess of things?

Certainly he had not pursued success by way of a conventional career. But he had found in himself a vein of talent and, over the years, had cultivated it with diligence and success. And this, in its way, was better than using his birth and name to achieve, as he might have done, a mediocre position in the City. He had exploited his friends gaily and sometimes ruthlessly, but in return he had given his companionship and his talent lavishly. In the final analysis, who could say which of the two had given or received the most, Castlerosse or Beaverbrook? But in an association like theirs there could, happily, be no final analysis. Those who mourned Valentine on that autumn day in 1943 were aware, too, that something more than a bravura performance had finished. The era in which such a rich and grotesque personality as he could emerge to flout, scandalize and animate social life – that, too, was passing. The future, it seemed, would be less garish and more grey.

Index